The Miniature Horse

by
Jill Swedlow Coffey

Glastonbury Press
Ojai, California

THE MINIATURE HORSE

Address inquiries to:
GLASTONBURY PRESS
P.O. Box 1750
Ojai, CA 93024

First Printing 1984
Second Printing 1987
Third Printing 1992

Published in the United States of America

Library of Congress Cataloging-in-Publication Data:

Coffey, Jill Swedlow, 1942-
        The miniature horse / by Jill Swedlow Coffey. -- 2nd ed.
                p.   cm.
        Summary: Discusses the history, care, training, and breeding of miniature horses.
                ISBN 0-944963-03-X : $22.95 -- ISBN 0-944963-02-1 (soft) : $16.95
                1. Miniature horses. [1. Miniature horses. 2. Horses.]
        I. Title.
        SF293.M56C64   1991
        636.1--dc20   91-40752
                                                                CIP
                                                                AC

The Miniature Horse

Photographs

Our cover photograph is by Thomas Nebbia whose photographs have graced the pages of many national and international magazines. His work has appeared frequently in National Geographic magazine since 1959. The comprehensive article on "Miniature Horses" that appeared in National Geographic (Vol. 167, #3, March 1985) featured photographs that were all taken by Thomas Nebbia.

All of the color photos that appear in Chapter One: "A Brief History" were taken by Thomas Nebbia.

All of the color photographs that appear in Chapter Eleven: "Foaling" were taken by the Author.

Most of the black and white photos that appear in the book were taken by the Author.

A number of the black and white photos were contributed by other miniature horse enthusiasts. We have noted their names where known. Page 5, Carol Trecker, Downey, CA Pages 28, 65, 149, "Whinney."

This book is dedicated to my father, Dave Swedlow, who never failed to encourage me in any endeavor I had undertaken. His love was never doubted, and his support was always there.

The Miniature Horse

TABLE OF CONTENTS

A BRIEF HISTORY

It would seem that the mists of time have engulfed any records of the first occasion a breeder deliberately set out to shrink horses down to the size of a small Great Dane dog.

The fact remains, however, that perhaps as long ago as the Sixteenth Century, someone did just that. One source, a reprint from the old *International Miniature Horse Journal* states that there is evidence of the existence of very small horses in the Far East as early as 3,000 B.C. However, they were probably dwarfed due to their living in a very harsh environment. In any case we have living proof in our present day Miniature Horses that it is definitely possible to produce very tiny horses.

According to the *International Miniature Horse Registry Directory,* the first Miniature Horses were bred by the royal courts of Europe as pets and playmates for the young princes and princesses of the day. To quote the above mentioned directory:

"The ingenuity of the Renaissance Period was required to create this breed. For score upon score of years, the stature of the horse was gradually reduced from full size by some of the most selective breeding techniques ever practiced. The trusted royal stable manager was very influential and highly respected for his skills and knowledge—he was practically a member of the Royal Court. Everything he needed was supplied as the Royal Stables were considered a national treasure."

It is probably not unreasonable to assume that the breeders of the distant past used basically the same selection techniques to diminish size which we incorporate today. Initially selecting the smallest equines available, they bred the smallest to the smallest, keeping only those foals exhibiting smaller size than their parents at maturity.

In attempting to set any trait, especially in the establishment of a "new breed," inbreeding becomes essential. I would guess that probably many sister/brother matings took place and perhaps, as smallness became predictable, mother to son and father to daughter was not an uncommon practice.

Certainly these inbreedings must have produced their share of dwarves, inherited deformities, and other undesirable traits; but they achieved their purpose too. These very small, adequately conformed, Miniatures were used to perpetuate the breed. They were the ones which bred true. In other words, their babies were well conformed because genetically they were free of the undesirable traits. (See the chapter on Genetics—Basis of All Inheritance, for further explanation).

The results of such a breeding program are not realized in ten, twenty or perhaps even 100 years. So it is easy to appreciate the tragic loss which almost occurred as kingdoms lost their wealth and power, and the little horse began to be dispersed.

They were sold to circuses which roamed the countryside and probably to other sources even less savory. Circuses in those days were not noted for the good care their animals received. The creatures were a means to earn money and most were maintained on the minimum of care and feed which would sustain life. The miniature horses were treated no differently than their fellow inmates, and there probably were no breeding programs of any consequences.

As the huge circuses began to decline, the remaining miniature horses were probably sold off to whoever had the price. The many European wars and the First World War did nothing to promote the breed either. I think it is safe to assume that any records which had existed are now gone and will probably never be found. Fortunately some of the Minatures themselves did survive and as early as the 1800's a few entered the United States with shiploads of imported horses from Europe.

One of the earliest enthusiasts in America was Moormon Field. He had spent a lifetime loving and raising horses. One of his enterprises was the importation of ponies from Europe to be used as the draft animals in the coal mines of Virginia. Occasionally these shipments would include very small animals. In those days they were referred to as midget ponies. Moormon kept these appealing equines and began breeding them.

Some of them were also used in the mines. No longer the pampered pets of royalty, the exiled waifs were now employed as draft stock. Their smaller size but great strength allowed them to be used in the smaller mine tunnels. It is a great credit to the breed itself that these tiny horses were sturdy enough to work and thrive under conditions which were certainly far from healthy.

In 1946, a Mr. Stewart from Canada saw a chance to make a profit from Miniature Horses. He spent six months in Holland, where they seemed to be plentiful, and bought about 200 Miniature Horses. In 1947 he held an auction in Orange, Virginia with 120 head for sale.

Moorman Field bought about 20 of the smallest mares at an average price of $750.00 per horse. At his peak, Moorman owned around 50 Miniature Horses. When Moorman died in 1964 at the age of 75, his son Tom continued the breeding operation for several years, and then sold all but one favorite mare and stallion, which they still owned at the time of publication of the first edition of this book.

In the 1950's, Smith McCoy of Rodderfield, West Virginia was looking for a hobby and became interested in the Miniature Horse. He decided to buy every one he could find under 32 inches in height. His search took him thousands of miles back and forth across the United States.

He finally located 10 or 12 horses which fit his requirements. From this very small beginning he eventually built a herd of 100 horses, the smallest of which was a 27 1/2 inch black mare. In those days height was measured at the top of the withers instead of the bottom of the mane as we do today!

In the late 1960's Smith, suffering from rheumatoid arthritis, was forced to sell the bulk of his herd. He held a sale in Tagewell, Virginia in September of 1967. The sale drew approximately 200 people from 10 different states. The average price was $400.00 and top price was $950.00 for a black stallion. He kept 20 head but eventually sold all but 5 and moved to Marion, Virginia, where he was still living in 1984, having finally sold even these last 5 horses.

Moorman Field and Smith McCoy probably have the distinction of having the largest early herds in the United States but the imports from South America have also played their part in this breed.

In the early 1800's, in Argentina, a man named Julio Falabella became interested in breeding very small horses. Some of his foundation stock came from the herd of the Hope sisters in England. Their breeding program was possibly the only early one which followed the planned breeding practices which produced consistently high quality miniature horses.

There seems to be some discrepancy about the true origins of the Falabella herd. Many articles about Julio Falabella's horses state that they were bred down from Arabians and Thoroughbreds but since Falabella refused to divulge his breeding secrets, one can only speculate. One story has it that he saw a "dwarf" horse drinking from a brook and that this was his foundation sire. It should be clarified here that contrary to some people's belief, Falabella horses were not a breed apart from the other Miniatures. They were simply a distinct genetic line bearing the farm name of Falabella.

A gentleman named John Aleno owned a farm adjoining Falabella's in Argentina. They were very good friends and it was because of this that Julio finally agreed to sell a few of his horses to Aleno.

The horses were sent to America deep in the hold of a ship, but upon arrival were rejected by the authorities because they had developed a skin fungus from the many days in the damp hold. They were returned to Argentina where they recovered and were then reshipped to the United States—this time by air!

John Aleno used his small herd as a promotional gimmick for the Regina Winery in Etiwanda, California. They were referred to as Lillaputian Horses. They pulled a scaled-down stagecoach with the winery's crest on it and appeared in many parades. They were also available for viewing by the public.

When John Aleno died, the bank took over the horses as part of his estate. They were subsequently sold to a Mr. Fuller who had

600 acres of land in Running Springs, California. He had the idea of turning his land into a recreation area and incorporating the Miniatures into the park. Unfortunately, some barriers were encountered when permission was needed to build an access road through government land.

The horses had been kept on a 300 acre ranch in Carbon Canyon, California. The herd increased, but a planned breeding program was not used. However, since no outside stock was brought in, the Falabella strain was kept pure. Since their dream of having a recreational park was impossible, the Fullers sold their horses.

One of the most frequent questions asked by novices and established breeders alike is: "What part does pony stock play in this breed?"

In my opinion, it plays a very significant role. I think it would be naive to blatantly state that no ponies have ever been used in the breed, although there are some who believe this.

Evidence that they have been used in both the past and present is obvious in a large percentage of the population. One indication is the gene which produces the color referred to as "silver dapple." To quote directly from the book *Equine Genetics and Selection Procedures* published by Equine Research Publications, Page 263:

> "The term silver dapple is frequently used to describe horses with an almost black to light milk-chocolate coat color and a silver mane and tail, frequently accompanied by a dark 'mask' on the face. The silver dapple gene may also cause dappling on chestnuts, sorrels, etc., but is more commonly associated with the liver and black coat colors which become light milk-chocolate to almost black with silver dapples. Silver dapple is due to a dominant mutation within the Shetland Pony breed, first seen in 1886. The mutation occurs only in Shetland Ponies and in horses with Shetland ancestry."

The above quote also seems to imply that any horse with dappling carries pony genes, but I think this is incorrect. A purebred dapple gray Arab certainly does not derive it's color from the Shetland. This would seem to be a different set of genes. Probably they should have been a bit more careful in their choice of words.

15

Other typical pony characteristics which regularly show up in the Miniature Horse are the very heavy and exceedingly long manes and tails; short, thick, cresty necks; heavy and excessive winter hair coats; and the ease of maintenance and pre-disposition to founder common to the Shetland breed.

In the case of Mini's with Appaloosa characteristics, mature height is much more difficult to keep down than in non-Appaloosa stock. Could this perhaps be due to the color having been derived from a fairly large pony breed known as the POA?

The intent here is not to point the finger of accusation at the early breeders but simply to point out that very probably the Shetland pony and other pony breeds have had their share of influence on the breed of the Miniature Horse. Knowing what is hidden in our breed's genetic closet is one of the first steps to breed improvement.

Because I could locate no truly accurate *documented* evidence to substantiate Miniature Horse history, the preceding information should not be taken as gospel. My sources were breed journals, reprinted newspaper and magazine articles as well as "word of mouth." The information accumulated had many of the characteristics of traditional stories which are verbally handed down from generation to generation. Tales which take this form of transmission often have information added or subtracted by the teller. However, they also may contain a good portion of factual information. Since each source yielded essentially the same stories, I feel there is good reason to believe the foregoing is fairly accurate.

Only 16" high, a new colt balances on his trainer's arms.

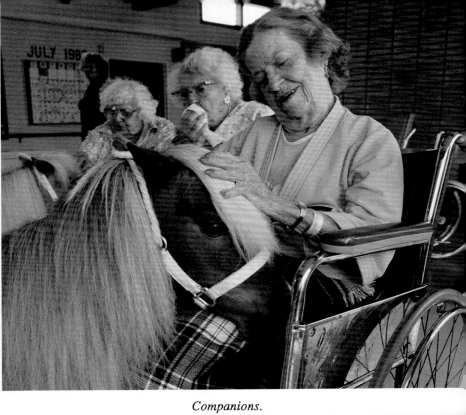

Companions.

A full grown mini sees eye to eye with a Saint Bernard dog.

Award winning breeder, Sister Bernadette, with Little Hot Shot of Monastery Mini Horse Ranch, which supports itself in part by raising miniature horses. Little Hot Shot was purchased for $17,500 and his sire brought $30,000.

A young foal is fed in the kitchen in this So. Carolina home.

... at work!

Taking a break.

A full grown 30" stallion gets ready, including his sneakers, for costume class at a competition in Dallas, Texas.

Although very similar to their larger counterparts, their size and unique traits make caring for a miniature horse special.

Palomino type miniature.

Paul Bunyan of Shadow Oaks Farms, California.

Miniature horse pulling a cart along side a Morgan horse.

WHAT IS A MINIATURE HORSE?

"What are they good for?" is very probably the most frequently asked question regarding Miniature Horses. It's a little like asking what good is a pet dog or cat. Basically they are pets, lovable tiny equines (not over 34 inches tall) which give a great deal of pleasure. However, unlike dogs and cats, they fulfill a different niche.

For people with horse mania, limited room, limited income and a burning desire to breed and show horses, this is the breed for them. Unlike their larger cousins, they do not destroy the food budget. Eight miniatures can be maintained in a very healthy condition on the same amount of hay as a large horse. They do not need as much room as large horses. I know of at least one lady who has bootlegged her stallion into a very exclusive, non-horse neighborhood and exercises him in the swimming pool!

27

One of the most endearing traits of the Miniature Horse is their temperament. They behave more like a faithful, curious dog than a horse. They seem especially fond of children and can *usually* be trusted to neither bite nor kick. (Very young children should not be left unattended with a Miniature just as a precaution.) Their curiosity knows no bounds. One of my young mares inspects and will eat anything I toss out to the chickens including raw eggs, egg shells and garden snails. (The above is not a recommended diet!) It is not unusual to find one standing in my large manure cart, apparently needing the higher elevation to catch a cooling breeze, or perhaps just needing a new activity. I've heard of putting the cart before the horse but never the horse in the cart! I have one who would happily ride around in the cart while I fill it with manure, but I draw the line at that one.

Because of their wonderful disposition, they're ideal for the handicapped or those confined to a wheelchair. Chair-bound owners are welcomed in the ring to show their own horses. The elderly

handle them with equal ease adding new dimensions to late life that might be impossible with full sized horses. They are easily trained to pull a cart and most can pull two adults with ease. Small children can ride them and many shows provide lead-line classes for the kids.

Perhaps one of their most appealing qualities is their salability. This is one of the reasons I began raising them. Although larger colts are a dime a dozen, the mares and fillies are worth their weight in gold. Hopefully the continued promotion of gelding stock will rectify this situation with the colts since the larger gelding really makes the best driving horse and pet.

Small, well conformed stallions and colts are also valuable. Because they are economical to raise and their prices are usually high, they are capable of providing their owner with a very decent income. It should be kept in mind, however, that even if you are starting this as a business, breed improvement should be your primary goal. There is enough genetic garbage floating throughout the breed at present. It may take you a bit longer to achieve your goals but there is always a market for good quality and it will be worth your effort in the end. Breed promotion and improvement should be our only goal right now.

Mini's are very intelligent and easily trained. One of mine was a nine-month-old baby, still running with her mother, having never been handled when I bought her. Within five days she was halter broken, stood tied, unconcernedly accepted a blanket, allowed her feet to be handled and cleaned and followed me around like a devoted puppy. I've never had a standard size foal advance that quickly even when they are handled from birth!

Miniature Horses are probably healthier as a group than standard horses. Although small, they are rugged and sturdy little guys. Given proper care, vaccination, worming and feed it is not uncommon for them to live routinely to 25 years of age and often longer. They can never replace a standard size horse for those who love to ride, but I dare say they will be ranked among the more popular breeds of the future.

HOUSING A MINIATURE HORSE

I wish to make it clear that this chapter title does not mean that your Miniature should share your house with you.

I have yet to see documented evidence that horses can be housebroken. This doesn't mean that he can't come in for an occasional visit. I think that's one of the first things a new Mini owner does—it is so utterly preposterous to have a horse in your house....and such FUN!! One of my very first ones had occasional run of the house and delighted in emptying the dishwasher of its pots and pans. She also liked to pull all the towels off their racks in the bathroom.

When your little horses aren't cantering through the living room, they need their own quarters. Since they're so small, their accommodations are a bit different from those for a larger horse.

Security Fencing

Security for your Miniature Horse is as important a consideration as shelter. Their small size and appeal make them prime targets for theft and objects of fun for stray dogs and thoughtless children.

The vision of 2 1/2 foot high white board fences is terribly appealing, but it will do little to protect your horses. A fence made of 6 foot high 'V' mesh wire is the ideal, possibly topped with a strand or two of barbed wire if you're really paranoid. The second choice would be chain link although I've seen little feet get caught in chain link. The main consideration is keeping predators of all kinds out as much as keeping the horses in. Quite probably you will only need to use 6 foot high fencing as your perimeter fencing, but be certain that you periodically check it for security.

I learned this lesson in a tragic way. One day I was cleaning stalls and heard some commotion in the pasture. I looked up in time to watch two stray dogs chase my terrified six month old filly smack into a cement block wall where she fell dead with a broken neck. Apparently she was so frightened that she didn't see the wall in time. Needless to say I have become paranoid about the safety of my horses. The dogs had slipped through a rather large hole under the fence. They probably dug it themselves, but I'll never know because I had assumed all was secure.

I'd like to say a word about dogs and horses here. I'm even careful about my own dogs with the horses. I have Great Danes which I breed and show. I had the dogs long before I had Miniature Horses so the dogs were not raised with the Mini's. I've seen the dogs pack together and run the fence line which separates them from the Mini's when the Mini's start playing. I believe that almost any breed of dog would pack up in excitement and chase a frightened Miniature Horse or worse. The pack instinct can take over in a flash and tragedy

can result. Unless your dog is a trustworthy herding breed and you **KNOW** he's reliable with your horses, please do not leave him unsupervised with your horses.

Corral and barn area

Interior Fencing

The individual corrals and cross fencing will probably not need to be any higher than 2 1/2 to 3 feet in height. However, in the case of a stallion, 4 feet is probably minimum height.

Wooden post and rail is a good material in every aspect, except that horses like to chew wood. If you own an avid wood fancier, your fence will soon look as if it had been under attack by an army of giant termites.

If you do use wood, please avoid redwood. Redwood contains tannic acid which can irritate a chewing mouth—not enough to end the chewing unfortunately. If you have ever had a redwood splinter you know how painful a splinter would be to your horse and these pointers have also been known to cause tetanus.

When spacing your rails, keep in mind that a newborn foal does not need much room to roll under the base board. You might also want to remember that spaces between rails make great places to stick a head through and rub the mane. Holes in your horses' manes won't help them in the show ring.

Custom-made, scaled down portable pipe corrals are probably my favorite. If the top rail is low enough for the horses to put their head over, they won't be so tempted to rub their manes. The corrals can be made to any specification.

Wire or chainlink can be used too, but keep in mind the fact that little feet can get caught. A wood or metal panel along the lower 2 feet will go far to prevent this.

Do not use barbed wire unless it is only to top an existing fence. Too many injuries occur with barbed wire.

Each horse should have access to shelter within their corral or pasture. Any type of solid structure with a roof is fine. Better yet would be a three-sided shed with it's opening facing away from the prevailing winds.

Box Stalls

The general consensus of the breeders responding to my questionnaire (see Chapter Eight) was that the average size box stall for a Miniature Horse should be at least 8' x 8'. Mine are 8' x 5' with removable partitions to make them large enough for foaling. However, most of my horses are put in only at night or during wet and/or during very cold weather. They get plenty of exercise during the day. My show horses are in stalls during the day to prevent the sun from bleaching their coats. They are put outside at night for exercise.

If the horse is staying in a stall 24 hours daily then I would even suggest 10' x 10' as a minimum size box stall. Make sure your door and gate latches are secure and lockable with a harness snap. These little imps can be real escape artists. While you are at it, make sure that your feed room is secured with proper locks. Little 'escapees' can be very greedy if they find the grain supply and the last thing you need is a colicky or foundered horse. Do not ever use a padlock on a stall—they are death traps in case of a fire.

Barns vs. Pasture or Corral

For my own horses, I've found that a combination of box stall and corrals work best. During the day they have a large yard where they can exercise. And I have outdoor corrals should I need to separate them. During the rain or on cold, damp nights, they are kept inside. Most breeders responding found this to be ideal for their stock also. Do what works best for your particular situation.

Before you decide where to keep your new friend or friends, let me assume you already have one or two Miniatures and you're about to introduce a new arrival to the others.

DO NOT just turn the new arrival in with the other horses. Horses have a pecking order. Some are dominant and some subordinate. Often, in determining these social positions among themselves, much kicking and biting is employed and someone could get hurt. Put the new arrival in a corral where he can see his new roommates, and they can get acquainted with a barrier between them—while being able to touch noses—they'll be unable to land any kicks and can easily move away from a bite. Keep them together under supervision until you're sure everyone will get along.

Large, enclosed herd set-up

35

Once in a while you'll find that no matter what you do, you'll have one horse who is always picking on another. I had this happen when I brought home both a six month old filly and a three year old mare. My two year old mare took an instant dislike to both and when a few days of separation had passed and I tried putting everyone together, the two year old cornered the three year old and tried to kick the stuffing out of her. They never did get along and so I keep them separated at all times.

CARING FOR YOUR MINI

Feeding—A Mini Menu

The feed requirements for a Miniature Horse are the same as for a big horse—only less is required. The basic diet consists of baled hay or processed hay in pellet or cube form. They will also need: oat hay, grain (to supplement), vitamins, and minerals.

The type of hay you feed will often depend on what is available. I've found a diet of half alfalfa and half oat hay to be ideal. I have not had one case of colic with this diet. I would suggest you continue feeding whatever the breeder fed your horse before you bought him and later change him over slowly to a new diet, if you so desire.

Alfalfa hay should be bright green, smell fresh, and be as full of alfalfa leaves as possible. Avoid hay which is moldy, dusty, or composed mainly of coarse stems. Watch for any foreign objects or weed stickers within a bale.

I prefer to feed hay by weight. That way, I know exactly what each horse is getting and I can adjust the amount up or down as needed. The amount used to feed depends on the size, weight and use of each horse. My seven month old filly who weighs approximately 100 pounds, stays in good weight on 1 pound of hay morning and night, and one cup of Ace-Hi Oat Base; she also gets vitamins and minerals at night. My 13 year old pregnant mare who weighs around 275 to 300 pounds get 3 1/2 pounds of hay morning and night, plus 2 cups of grain mix and vitamins.

I would suggest feeding the same amounts the breeder you bought the horse from fed the mini and then adjust up or down depending on how the horse's weight changes and how he looks. I always feel like I'm starving my little guys when I give them their minuscule

portions, but they gain weight so easily that I really must control my "Jewish-Mother" instinct.

Some breeders feel that feeding hay contributes to "hay bellies" and prefer to feed pelleted hay. One of my first Mini's, a yearling colt, had a very prominent hay belly. After consulting with a couple of breeder friends, I switched him from hay to pellets, feeding approximately the same poundage to start. (The horse was already on a regular worming program). When he showed no improvement after two weeks, I began to decrease the amount of pellets. All that happened was that his ribs began to show, but he continued to have a hay belly! He was thoroughly checked by my Vet and found to be slightly anemic. The anemia was treated, but there was still no improvement. He really seemed to be an inherently unthrifty animal. He was active and seemed healthy in all other respects. One breeder told me that the "Hay Belly" can sometimes be caused by the foal's cecum becoming active and that the enlarged belly will return to normal with age.

In my colt's case, pellets were not the answer, but many breeders feed them and find them highly satisfactory. If you do use them, do not buy the cheapest brand unless you know they are made from good quality hay. My feed dealer recently informed me that many pellets are composed of very poor quality alfalfa mixed 2 to 1 with straw! This is a real problem with pellets—you really don't know what you are getting. Another objection to pellets is that the horses eat them so quickly, they don't get all the chewing activity they require and take it out on the barn.

I have not encountered one breeder who feeds hay cubes to his Miniature Horses probably because they are too big for those little mouths to crunch. Maybe they would work, but I hesitate to recommend them. Their contents can be as difficult to be sure of as pellets.

Most breeders I have talked with said they fed some type of grain supplement. Here again the amount will vary with the size and use of the horse. I give one cup daily regardless of the size with the exception of my pregnant mares. When they enter the last trimester of their pregnancy, or have nursing foals, they get two cups of grain.

If you have never had horses before, be aware that an over abundance of grain can cause founder, colic, or even kill a horse of any size. Be careful here. If you are in doubt about the amount of feed, consult your Veterinarian. Shetland ponies are especially susceptible to founder, and I suspect the same is true of Miniature Horses.

If your horse is getting good quality hay, a little grain, has a mineralized salt block available and is only a pet, he probably does not need a vitamin / mineral supplement. But I would suggest giving a good all-around vitamin / mineral supplement to animals being used for breeding and for showing. Since there are literally hundreds of products available, I once again suggest you consult the breeder or your Veterinarian. My personal preference is to use a natural product which provides all the vitamin / mineral requirements and does not contain any antibiotics. Read the label and know what you are getting. I usually quarter the dosage recommended for standard horses for a Mini. Just sprinkle it on top of the grain ration.

Don't fall victim to the belief that if a little is good, more is better. More damage is done to young growing animals by overfeeding and over-use of vitamins and minerals than you would believe. *Balance* is the key to good nutrition. The only reason I feed vitamins at all is to cover the possible lack of nutrients in the soil on which the feed is grown.

Visiting the garden!

40

All horses need free access to salt. I use the mineralized blocks that contain iodine and plunk them in the bottom of their mangers. Check the salt supply from time to time since they will often go through it very quickly. Salt blocks which are exposed to water can dissolve overnight in a heavy rainstorm.

Fresh, clean water should be available at all times. Use large buckets or automatic waterers. I prefer the automatic waterers that work on the float principle like a toilet tank. I am not sure a young foal would be strong enough to depress the paddle type waterer. Check all water receptacles daily to make sure they function. Check also for dirt and manure which occasionally gets deposited in the waterer.

I like to give my horses treats from time to time in the form of carrots, apples or fresh green grass. Just don't overdo the amounts. Sugar is a no-no! It is as bad for horses as it is for people.

Grooming on a Small Scale:

Clipping a Mini

It is not my intention here to go into great detail on how to hold a brush when you groom or to list what each grooming utensil is used for. There are many good books available on horse care in general which will help you. I will touch on subjects which concern Miniatures specifically. If you have owned standard size horses, you already know most of what is needed, a great deal of the rest is common sense.

Owning an unclipped Mini in the winter is a little like living with a walking dust mop. If you have just acquired the horse, you probably won't be able to keep yourself from body clipping him so you can see what you bought. Before getting the clippers out, there are a few things to consider.

If you live in a cold winter area and it is December, *don't clip,* especially if your new horse is a baby. Even if you blanket, the shock of losing all the insulation of that heavy coat could cause your horse to become ill. However, if you live in a mild winter area, you will probably do no harm by clipping the coat as long as you provide a warm blanket as a substitute. If your horse has come from a cold winter area to Southern California, you'll probably be doing him

Here is one of my mares before clipping

Same mare as above, after clipping!

a favor. Even if you decide to leave the coat you might want to trim the long hair on the fetlocks to prevent mud and dirt build-up.

As in all breeds, Miniature Horses will shed out their coats naturally as the days grow longer and warmer in the Spring. If you are not faced with an early show, you are much better off to allow the coat to shed out naturally. The hair color will be brighter and shinier than if clipped.

If you decide to body clip, here is what you need. One large horse clipper (such as a Sunbeam) and a smaller clipper with a set of number 10 and a number 30 blades. The Oster A5 clipper is what I prefer, but there are many good makes available.

Before starting, wash the horse thoroughly. Do not do this on a cold day because that shaggy coat will take a long time to dry and your horse could become ill. A dirty coat will not cut easily and will dull your blades quickly. And, by the way, do not clip until the coat is *thoroughly* dry.

Have clipper oil and/or a silicon spray to keep the blades working smoothly. Have a can of one-half kerosene and one-half motor oil mixed together to clean the blades of your large clippers. Dip the blades in the mix while the clippers are running. Check the temperature of the blades with your hand so you don't burn your horse.

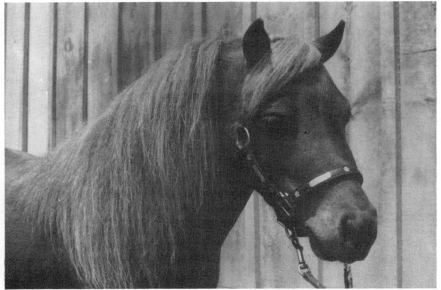

Unless your horse accepts the clipping calmly and has no fear, it is best to have an assistant, especially when clipping in tricky places like under the front legs. One person can pull a front leg forward stretching out the arm-pit skin for safer, easier clipping.

If you are clipping a baby or any horse for the first time, go slow and be patient. The horse will be frightened until he realizes that the clippers won't hurt him. Even a veteran may have to be eared down (holding the ear in a folded, bent in half position) or tightly held in order to clip his ears.

Start with the small clippers and the number 10 blades on the face, clipping against the hair growth. Clean the face and head of all hair except for the forelock of course. Be especially careful around the eyes. Do not trim the hair from the inside of the ears unless you are clipping for show. The hair protects the ear from bugs and dirt.

The feet are most easily cleaned up with the smaller clippers and the number 10 blades. You may even find it easier to do the entire leg with the small clippers because of all the nooks and crannies.

Then use your larger clippers to finish the body. Use long firm strokes to avoid streaks.

Clipping along the crest can be tricky, especially with a very fuzzy baby. Separate the mane from the fuzz as best you can with a comb one section at a time. Then, using the small clippers and a number 10 blade, clip very carefully along each side of the mane. Determine how long you want the bridle path and clip this with the number 10 blades.

To finish off, snap on your #30 blades and re-clip the muzzle; and if you are showing, clean the inside ear and nostrils of all hair. You will find it easier to reach all the hair in the nostrils if you gently slide the skin under the nostril down toward the muzzle. This exposes all the hair within the nostril for easy access.

Re-bathe the horse to remove all loose hair and follow up with a cream rinse or, better yet, an Alpha Keri and water rinse to help restore the body oils. Use 1 capful of Alpha Keri per gallon of warm water.

Foot Care
The feet of your Miniature need special consideration. Shoes are not needed but correct trimming is. Few laymen are qualified to

trim feet, although apparently many do. My farrier (proper name for your horse shoeing professional) has shown me how to trim mine, but so far I have been too "chicken" to try it. The last time he trimmed my horses, he showed me again what to do, and I am going to try to file them soon. I also intend to purchase and study a good book on farrier work.

All I can say on this subject right now is that I suggest you have your farrier out and ask his advice about doing it yourself. If you feel confident and want to try, more power to you! Since I have seen so many standard sized horses nearly crippled by improper trimming, I have been afraid of doing my horses some harm.

Miniature Horse feet do need cleaning to prevent thrush, or foot rot. I have found that picking them out every other day is sufficient for good foot health. If the hoof horn appears dry you can buy good hoof preparations in most feed stores which will help keep

the moisture in the hoof. It is best to soak the feet in water to rehydrate them. Let them dry and then apply the hoof preparation. Most hoof oils only keep the hoof from losing moisture, they *do not* add moisture. My favorites are Fieblings Hoof Oil and Aloe Hoof.

Brushing
Brushing your Mini's coat daily is, of course, ideal. However, the more horses you have, the more difficult this becomes. Unless I have one I'm actively showing—or they are all shedding like crazy—I try for a once weekly, thorough grooming.

Shedding

Until the hair follicles decide the time has come to give up the ghost, there is little that can be done to make a winter coat or foal hair let go. (Extending the daylight artificially under electric bulbs might be helpful, but I've never tried it.)

However, once the coat has begun to shed there are a few things you can do to hurry it along. Daily use of a rubber curry comb, used in a circular motion, will pull out all the dead hair. Shedding blocks are really helpful too, and the horses really enjoy this.

Bathing the horse with warm water is helpful followed by vigorous use of the rubber curry comb after the coat is dry. I am not convinced that the practice of keeping a winter blanket on a horse makes any difference except to hold the coat flatter to the body.

One process that really helps once the shedding has begun is to do the following:

Make a solution of one cup Alpha Keri Lotion (available from the drug store) in one gallon of very warm water. Take a sponge and saturate the coat with the solution and leave it on the coat overnight. The next day make a solution of one part Bubbling Bath Oil with Coconut Oil to two parts very warm water, and lather the coat thoroughly. Leave this on overnight. Repeat the above two more times. Then bathe the horse thoroughly with the bubbling bath oil, and rinse off every trace of soap. When the coat is dry use the rubber curry comb to pull out the loose hair. If needed this can be repeated.

If you think your horse may be sensitive to the oils, test a small area of his skin first. If you would prefer not to leave the products on him overnight, oil him in the morning and soap him in the early afternoon. Leave the solution on him for a couple of hours and then rinse him off. Repeat as often as needed.

Health Care

Vaccinations

When it comes to equine illness, prevention is the best cure. A good vaccination program can prevent Veterinarian bills and tragedy. For some strange reason, some breeders of Miniature Horses claim that certain vaccinations which work on standard horses are dangerous to a Miniature Horse. This contention has not been proven by any scientific method with which I am familiar. Until it is, I will continue to follow my Vet's advice about vaccinating my horses.

Your horses should have protection against tetanus, flu, rhino and perhaps the three strains of encephalitis. In some areas it might be advisable to include inoculations for rabies and strangles. Have your Veterinarian set up a program for your horses.

I know of a couple of instances where breeders refused to inoculate their pregnant mares against rhinopneumonitis. They couldn't understand why their mares aborted their babies or why the foals died soon after. Rhino is a notorious killer of unborn foals and is highly contagious. A simple vaccine serves to prevent it in most cases.

If you have many horses, you might want to administer your own vaccines in order to save money. Have your Vet or a knowledgeable friend instruct you in how to do this. If not done properly you risk injuring your horse. The dosage for Mini's is the same as the dose for a standard horse. Regardless of whether you are vaccinating a foal or a mature Mini give the full dose. Vaccinations are determined by a set dose not the animal's weight.

Worming

A good worming program is essential to good equine health. There is, however, a great deal of controversy about tube worming a Miniature Horse. Once again, your Veterinarian is your best advisor. I know of one Veterinarian who is also a Mini breeder who tubes his Mini's with no problem using a foal tube.

Regardless of method, your Mini should be paste wormed every 6 to 8 weeks. Since I am not a qualified Veterinarian, I will refer you again to your own Vet. Set up a program as to which product to use, frequency of product rotation and then stick to it religiously.

Please be careful of the products you use, some are not recommended for pregnant mares or young foals. Be sure to dose by weight recommendations on the product.

Teeth

When your Veterinarian is out for routine worming or vaccines, be sure to have him check the teeth of your older horses (probably from the age of four or five on). As a horse ages, he can get rough or uneven edges on his molars, especially if his bit is off. This can prevent the teeth from occluding (meeting) properly, and the food is not chewed thoroughly. This causes the stomach to work harder to digest the food. In turn, this can be a cause of colic or unthriftiness since the horse does not get the full nutrition from his ration.

If the teeth become very rough, they can cause the horse pain while he is chewing his food. Naturally, he will not be as enthusiastic about eating and will probably drop weight.

This is obviously not a complete guide to general horse care, nor is it intended to be. I encourage anyone not familiar with horse care to invest in a basic and thorough book on the subject if you are just learning.

PURCHASING A MINI FOR PET, SHOW OR BREEDING

The purchase of your first Miniature Horse would hardly seem to be a major problem at first glance. You have the money, you locate a breeder or dealer and go buy one.

Unfortunately for the first time buyer that is usually exactly what happens. And, what is even sadder is that the buyer is often very sincerely interested in breeding or showing and may end up with an animal unsuitable for anything other than a pet. There are steps to follow and things to know which can aid you in obtaining a suitable horse for your purpose. It may take a little longer and take a little more effort on your part, but it is well worth the extra time and trouble.

Know What You Want

First of all, what is your intention in owning a Miniature Horse? If you are only looking for a pet there is less to know than if you are looking for a show or breeding prospect. However, before you buy *any* horse, you should locate a "reputable" breeder.

How Do You Locate a "Reputable" Breeder?

The old saying "buyer beware" applies just as strongly in horse buying as in any other category—probably more so. If you have had NO experience with livestock of any kind, you would be wise to attend as many Miniature Horse Shows as possible (A list can be obtained by writing to one of the Registries which are listed in

Chapter 14). Study the Breed Standard until you are thoroughly informed on good conformation as well as the disqualifying and serious flaws. Ask questions of exhibitors and breeders. In short, become as conversant with the breed as possible so you will know what you are looking at when you begin visiting the various farms. If possible, take a friend with you who is knowledgeable about horses.

As you visit each breeder, take note of the condition of the animals themselves. Are they generally in good health, carrying good weight, having no discharges from eyes or nose? Every breeder's herd has its bouts with colds or flu, but if after subsequent visits the horses always seem ill, I would suggest passing up that farm.

Ask what guarantees the breeder will extend with a sale. If you are buying a baby, will size be guaranteed? If you buy a colt, will they replace him if both testicles do not descend by a certain age? Do they know the pedigree of their sale stock? If you are buying future brood stock you should at least know what the parents, and better yet grandparents, look like. Will they allow you to check the horse's mouth for proper bite?

If a full grown adult is being purchased, will they allow you to personally measure the animal? This should be done with any adult you're considering! If you are buying a filly, will the breeder offer a breeding to one of their stallions when the filly is old enough? If you're purchasing a pregnant mare, will they rebreed her at no charge shold there be no foal or if she aborts? Are they willing to put all guarantees in writing?

I don't mean to insinuate that a breeder is disreputable if they do not do all of the above. Each breeder has a sales agreement which they feel works best for them, and it would be a rare person indeed who would guarantee all of the above. However, if a breeder extends no guarantee whatsoever, I would think twice before buying his stock.

A reputable breeder will be willing and able to point out the bad points of his horses as readily as he shows the good. Even the top winning show animal has a few faults. If you are planning on showing your purchase you will do the breeder, yourself, and the breed as a whole a disservice by showing an inferior animal. Breeders who care about the breed know this and are anxious that you buy a really good specimen.

As you travel from breeder to breeder, ask as many questions as you can. You will begin to get a feel for which ones are truly con-

Draft Type

51

cerned with the breed and those who are not. Don't be impatient and rush into a purchase, take your time to learn, and you will probably be much more satisfied with your final decision.

Why Are You Buying a Mini?

The next decision to be made is what you intend to do with your Miniature. This will have a bearing on what you can expect to pay and which qualities would be most important to look for. (See also Chapter 12.)

Oh, I Only Want a Pet

Now this seems like a simple, straightforward statement doesn't it? If you really do want only a pet and are *certain* you will never have an urge to show or breed, all well and good. However, if in your search for this pet, you have ever stood ringside and had a small twinge of envy while watching some happy exhibitor take first place in his class, you'd best reexamine your priorities. The chances are that once your pet has insinuated himself into your heart you will begin having fantasies of him winning in the show ring! Should you also decide to show the world that he is as good as the winners, you are probably going to be sorely disappointed. He was pet quality when you bought him and there has been no magical transformation simply because you love him. The only additional cost involved with owning a show-quality animal is the initial purchase price. It costs no more to feed a show horse than a pet, so be very certain of what the future may hold for your Miniature Horse and yourself.

If you decide you really want a pet quality Mini you must consider the following:

Which sex is best? First consider that a mare or filly of any quality will probably cost more than a gelding or colt. A gelding, or colt that you will have gelded, is by far the best choice. Even Miniature stallions can be nippy and less reliable temperament-wise than geldings or mares. I would not recommend trusting a stallion with children unsupervised.

(A special caution about Miniature Horses and children. Please be sure to supervise children in the company of a Miniature Horse. Even though he is small the Mini is still a member of the horse family and requires proper handling.)

A mare could be a good choice if you think you'll have her spayed. Although mares can sometimes be a little testy during their estrus cycles, this is not the reason I suggest spaying. Once she is spayed, you'll never have the option of breeding her, and if she is pet quality you will only be doing the breed a disservice in allowing her to reproduce her inferior qualities. The desire to have a baby Mini around can be a great temptation. If you're going to want to breed your mare, buy a good one!

So if you've considered well and still want a pet quality Mini, what do you look for? Health should be your first consideration, as it should with any horse regardless of use. To begin with, look for a pair of bright clear eyes, dry nostrils and alert attitude. There should be no discharge from the eyes, nostrils, ears, anus, vulva or penis. Manure or wetness evident under the tail or on the buttocks warrants further investigation. Manure should be firm and well formed. The coat should be bright and shiny even if the Mini's sporting their winter fuzz. Some breeders maintain large herds and if the horses have tangled manes and tails and some dirt in their coats, remember that there are only 24 hours in a day and it would be impossible to groom every horse daily. The body and legs should be free of any obvious lumps or injuries. There should be no limping or shuffling at any of the gaits.

If the horse under consideration is not a half-wild baby, his temperament will be obvious. I must say, however, that I have rarely seen or heard of a bad temperament in this breed. It is hard to go wrong here, even if the Mini is wild it will probably be acting like a puppy within a week of you getting it home.

Age is probably unimportant in a pet since these little horses live to a ripe old age. A 20 year old would probably be around for at least another 10 years and possibly more. However, a baby is such fun to watch grow up, they're so full of the devil! It is hard to go wrong here as well.

If your candidate passes all the above considerations, I strongly suggest you have the horse checked by your Vet. Most of the breeders I questioned felt the buyer could judge health, but unless you are a Veterinarian, you could be making a serious mistake. The Mini could have heart problems, respiratory problems or any type of unsoundness that a layman couldn't detect. Better to know this before your new friend comes home, steals your heart and runs up giant Vet bills or worse. No matter what purpose you intend for your horse,

I strongly urge that you make the finality of the sale contingent on a clean bill of health.

The Best Age For Breeding Stock

The dividing line between breeding and show quality mares is very narrow. A show quality horse is, or should be, good enough to breed. I believe that in the case of a stallion this should almost always be true. A stallion always exerts a greater influence on the gene pool as a whole because he can produce hundreds more offspring in his lifetime than a mare.

To be listed on the registration papers as the breeder, you must own the mare when she is bred. Therefore, a stallion ownership should not be your first priority when first establishing your herd.

Older Mares

Everything mentioned regarding health in looking for a pet applies to your selection of a brood mare and will not be repeated here. In addition to health, there are many other important traits to look for.

First let us consider age. By buying a mature mare, you take no risk of her going over the size limit and you know how she looks at maturity. However, there can be hazards in purchasing an older mare who is no longer a maiden (unbred) mare. One would first question why a breeder would sell a good brood mare when they are few and far between. Maybe she was one of their first acquisitions and they have since collected better quality mares. Maybe she is oversized but was registered prior to the registries closing and they no longer wish to use larger stock in their program. Maybe they have simply run out of room for so many horses or need some cash. The above reasons are certainly legitimate and you would probably be getting a good deal. However, mares are also sold because they are sterile, abort early, produce large foals, produce dwarves and are not good mothers. Buying a mare with these problems is no bargain for the buyer.

I would recommend buying an older mare only under the following circumstances:

1. You know and feel very confident about the breeder.
2. The mare passes a thorough Vet check.
3. You can see her offspring or pictures of same and their quality is acceptable, or she has a nice foal at her side.
4. If she is sold as being in foal, the breeder should guarantee a live foal or offer a free breeding back to one of her stallions.

Maiden Fillies Under Three Years Of Age

In the case of buying a filly foal there are also risks. First of all you have no assurance of her mature height. Even if the seller will guarantee height, you have wasted a fair amount of time waiting for her to grow up, should she go oversize. Next, you do not know what she will look like as a mature mare, babies can change a lot, especially if they are weanlings at time of purchase. You will also have to wait a season or so before you can breed her if she is very young.

On the plus side, you can be certain she is not being sold because of breeding problems, although that is no guarantee that she won't later have them. You are more likely to be able to see her parents than you would with an older mare. There will be more to choose from in this mare category than any other and that is a decided advantage.

I would suggest that you look primarily in this age group for your brood mare, but keep a sharp eye out for the next category.

Older Maiden or Young Bred Stock

Though few and far between, to say nothing of price, this is probably the ideal purchase. A long, two year old (or older) mare carrying her first foal would just about eliminate any risk to the buyer

Quarter Type Stallion

56

except the very real possibility of being thrown in debtor's prison after you have paid for her! With animals there is always a chance for the unexpected, but the chances are smallest here.

The older the mare, the more certain you are of her eventual height and conformation. A two or three year old maiden is certainly a good choice if you can find one.

Stallions—Which Age is Best?

The ideal stallion purchase would be an older proven animal with plenty of offspring you could see. Here there is no question of size, conformation or prepotency. The availability of such an animal may be better than one would expect since often a breeder has all the get (offspring) from a particular stallion that they wish to use in their breeding program.

In lieu of finding the above, the next age choice would be a three year old or older. Again, size and conformation are established. You know what you are getting physically. What he will produce genetically is still a question if he has no foals on the ground.

I do not recommend the purchase of a colt much younger than three years. Too many things can go wrong with a very young horse before he reaches maturity. Testicles can fail to descend and size is often unpredictable.

A Few Considerations Before Buying Brood Stock

Buying your foundation stock will be one of the most important steps you'll ever take as a breeder. Take as much time as you need to know the good and bad in overall conformation. See as many close relatives of the prospective purchase as possible. Be *very* selective.

Nothing has been mentioned as to price. The reason is because the prices fluctuate wildly from region to region and breeder to breeder. However, I strongly urge you to buy the very best you can afford, even if this means waiting a little longer. However, don't be fooled into thinking that the higher the price, the better the horse. I've seen several $10,000.00 animals I wouldn't take as a gift! As stated earlier, it costs no more to feed a good one than a bad one and it is usually true that like begets like. Starting with the very best quality just puts your breeding program that much further along.

Arabian Type

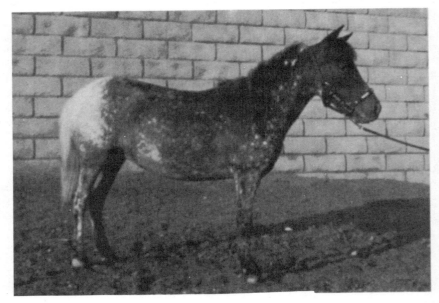

Appaloosa

58

Unless you are beginning with more than three or four mares, or live in an area where no top quality stallions are available, you probably don't need to buy a stallion right away. There are a large number of very nice stallions standing at public stud, and you can pick and choose the right one for your mare. This also give you the option of breeding to several different animals with your particular mare. You can always buy a stud later or one of your mares may produce a stud quality colt.

Decide what "type" of Miniature Horse you wish to breed. You will notice that some Mini's resemble Arabians, others Draft or Thoroughbreds, et cetera, in conformation. If you have a preference, you should buy animals of that type and then set the traits genetically so they breed true. (More on this in the chapter on Genetics).

The same applies to color preference. If you wish to breed pintos, buy pintos. If you want only chestnut or palomino colors, learn what phenotypes and genotypes produce these colors. If you detest certain colors, take the time to learn which gene combinations produce them and avoid these horses. There can always be surprises, as recessives can meet and produce the hidden trait in even the best planned matings, but forewarned is forearmed.

And while I am on the subject, do yourself and the breed a favor and learn at least the basics of genetic inheritance. There are many good books on the subject and if learned step-by-step, it is really quite understandable. You would not be able to create a sculpture without knowing how to use the tools—the same applies to livestock. I would also suggest you purchase *Equine Genetics and Selection Procedures*, by Equine Research Publications. If unavailable in your bookstore you will find it advertised in many horse publications such as Equus, Practical Horseman and many breed journals. It is not cheap, but it is a bargain at the price!

The Brood Mare

Some breeders claim that the brood mare contributes 51% to her foal while the stallion only contributes 49%. Anyone who knows genetics is aware that this is impossible, genetically speaking, but let's examine that statement a bit more closely.

The stallion contributes his sperm, the sperm carries his half of the foal's genetic make up and the stallion is now out of the picture. The mare, however, produces the ovum, nurtures the developing fetus in her body for eleven months, eleven days and then nurses and protects her baby until he is weaned. Her body determines the foal's health both in-utero and while nursing. Her maternal behavior protects and teaches him as a youngster. Genetics aside, the mare really does contribute more than only her half to the genetic makeup of her baby. Keep this in mind and never undervalue your mares.

Choosing Your Breeding Stock

The Mare

A broodmare should be free of any disqualifying fault. Her bite should be even with the jaw, being neither under nor overshot. She should not be a dwarf nor have any dwarf characteristics.

Stand back from her and view her from the side. You should get the impression of looking at a standard horse from a distance, overall proportions being correct.

The details of correct body conformation are included in almost any good book on horse conformation, so I will suggest that you become very familiar with correct structure and choose the horse which conforms most closely to this.

Since poor leg conformation is so prevalent in Mini's, do get a mare with the straightest legs possible. Her front feet should not toe in nor out, and avoid cowhocks behind. Clubfeet are also common and usually inherited so be careful if you're told her feet were not trimmed properly. Poor trimming *can* contribute to poor feet but this is not always the case and careful trimming can *hide* poor foot structure.

Also try to avoid a thick neck, steep croup and large coarse head. You'll have to allow a few faults because perfection doesn't exist in nature, but you'll have to decide which faults you can tolerate and which you cannot.

If you are purchasing your first mare, most breeders seem to agree that mares between 32 and 34 inches are least likely to have problems at foaling time. I, too have found this to be true and they can still produce smaller foals.

The Stallion

All of the above applies to buying a herd sire and then some. If you decide to use only your own stallion on all your mares, he should be of the best quality you can afford. Because his influence will be the greatest on your breeding program, especially if you plan to back cross his daughters to him.

Breeding Stock in General

Both stallions and mares should be able to move well and display general soundness. However, blemishes due to injury need not be considered as long as the horse is not handicapped as a breeding animal. Occasionally you may run across a horse that would be a top show prospect but for a disfiguring scar or injury. This could be a very good investment if the Vet check shows the animal capable of reproducing.

In conclusion, know what constitutes good conformation, take a knowledgeable friend with you. Buy the very best example of your preferred type you can afford from a breeder you trust, and have the horse thoroughly checked by a trusted Veterinarian. You have done all you can to give yourself a good start breeding Miniature Horses!

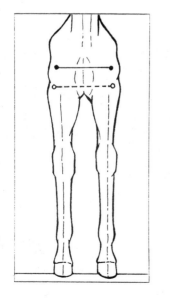

Ideal set of forelimbs as a whole is determined by the orientation of the arm bone (the bone spanning the distance between the point of the shoulder and the elbow). When the dashed line is the same length as the solid line, the whole forelimb is "set" to toe forward. If the lines are equal but the foal still toes in or out, there are offsets, rotations or deviations below the breast.

From the June/July 1988 issue of:
MODERN HORSE BREEDING
656 Quince Orchard Road
Gaithersburg, MD 20878

TRAINING AND HANDLING A MINI

This Chapter heading gives me amusing mental pictures of disciplining a Mini by picking it up and giving it a good shaking or rolling one onto its back to trim its feet. But even though they are little, remember a Miniature is still a horse! Their training is still the same as that given a standard sized horse; it is just easier and less dangerous to the trainer. Because there are many excellent texts on horse training available, I'm not going to get into great detail here, but will cover those subjects pertaining to Miniatures.

The training procedures are the same for an older, untrained horse as for a newborn Miniature. You will need to use a little more strength with the older horse, but with a new Mini be careful not to be too rough.

Remember, take your time, don't rush.

Once a newborn foal has established a relationship with its mother, usually during the first 24 hours, you may safely begin to get acquainted with the baby.

Move slowly and try not to startle or frighten the foal. Talk to him, touch him gently on all parts of his body to get him used to it. He will be skittish at first but will calm down when he realizes he is not being hurt.

If you cannot resist the temptation to pick the foal up, do it by placing one arm just under the points of his chest with the other arm under his buttocks. Do not pick him up under his stomach or chest as you could cause internal damage by compressing his organs.

I would suggest introducing him to a halter at a few days of age. First put the halter on and let him get used to the feel of it on his head. Make sure he is in an area where he cannot get the halter hooked on anything and even though you think the area is safe *do not leave him unattended.* A halter hooked on something can be a death trap.

After he has grown accustomed to a halter, snap on the lead rope and loop the free end around his rump to help him move forward. Give a gentle tug on the halter and a pull on the butt rope. One single step forward is reason enough for lavish praise. Keep at it until he will move freely by your side at the first pull on the halter, then you can dispense with the butt rope. If he falters, go back to the rope around his rear until he is leading reliably.

The one thing to remember with these little guys is their small size. Too strong a pull or jerk on the halter can easily injure a Miniature Horse, so be careful. If a horse or foal spooks or panics and abruptly pulls

64

away from you, go with him until he calms down enough for you to regain control.

When you first teach a Mini to stand tied use a quick release knot and find a location where he is not likely to hurt himself. A solid wall or large tree is ideal. If you decide to tie him to a chainlink fence, don't be surprised if in his struggles he breaks a leg by catching it in the fence.

Stay nearby so you can help should the horse really panic and get himself in trouble. You do not want him to rear up and get a leg caught over the rope or get himself into some other dangerous situation. Pulling back or moving from side to side is a natural reaction when the horse first feels himself to be restrained. As long as he is in no danger, allow him to pull all he wants. This is teaching him that he cannot escape and must stand quietly when tied. Be sure he is tied with a halter and rope which will not break or you will teach him he can escape whenever he wants.

After the initial lessons and when the horse begins to accept the fact that he must stay put, leave him tied up for increasingly longer periods of time. Perhaps you can leave him tied within your sight while you are cleaning the barn and corrals. Once he is standing calmly for an hour you can consider him to be trained to tie.

Once he ties well, start picking up each foot in turn and cleaning them out with a hoofpick. Groom him and generally get him used to all types of handling. Clippers can be introduced at this time in a gradual manner. Let him hear them running a few feet away from him. Then slowly move closer and, starting at the shoulder, run them over his body (not clipping) so he gets used to the feel of the vibration. Once he accepts this calmly, clipping can commence.

Show training for halter and harness classes is a subject which I am just beginning to learn. Try the library or bookstore where you will find some good books to learn from and look for my next book which will cover these subjects in detail. At the shows be observant and ask questions. Most exhibitors will be happy to help you as long as they are not hurrying to get into class.

TRANSPORTING A MINIATURE HORSE

Chauffeured Minis

When distances are too far for your Mini to walk, you will need to give some thought as to how you will transport him. Miniature Horses have been known to be transported in the back of Volkswagens and in the front seat of Cadillacs, but this becomes impractical on a routine basis.

The first method that comes to mind is a horse trailer. Most have removable dividers and the horses can be let loose, minus their halters. If only a couple of Mini's are being transported, they can be tied high enough so they cannot hook a leg over the rope. Or you could leave the divider in if it goes all the way to the floor. This allows you to carry up to two Miniature Horses loose on each side.

You could also remove the divider and build partitions for up to six horses. This would probably be the safest option. One problem that can occur with this method is if a halterless horse escapes when the door is opened, you may have a real problem recapturing him. He might run out onto a road and be hit by a car. Another difficulty is occasionally you will be required to unhitch your trailer at a show and park it away from the ring which can be very inconvenient.

Van with interior, custom tie stalls.

Innovative trailer, modified to transport Minis

The author's truck in which she transports her Minis

This little truck is really earning it's keep!

Compared to purchasing a truck or a van, a trailer is inexpensive especially if you can locate a used one.

My biggest objection to trailers is having to pull them. I am always nervous because I have less maneuverability in traffic and am basically at the mercy and the whim of other drivers, most of whom are very thoughtless about cutting in front of you or giving you room to change lanes. Wind, too, can be a hazard. I am also uneasy when I cannot keep an eye on the horses.

A van can easily be outfitted for horses and people alike but it has one huge disadvantage. The human passengers are subjected to breathing the same air that the horses copiously pollute as they travel! Horse manure in an enclosed space can be devastating. Bedding the van in shaving helps reduce the odor and gives the horses better footing.

The solution which works best for me is a truck with a shell. I have a 3/4 ton pick up and shell which has been outfitted inside with six removable tie stalls. The large sliding windows give plenty of ventilation, and there is a sliding window between the cab and the truck bed. The window can be opened if a horse needs help or reassurance and closed to protect the driver's nose from "essence of manure." The ramp has sides for safe loading and unloading when you have no assistance, and the whole thing folds flat and slides between the two sets of stalls for travel. I have full view of my horses at all times and full maneuverability of the truck.

Non-skid footing is essential for any vehicle in which you plan to convey your horses. I have found the best footing to be a combination of astroturf cut to fit the truck bed and secured with glued-on velcro strips underneath and about three inches of shavings spread on top. This allows me to remove the astroturf after each trip for thorough hosing down. Rubber mats are also good but some rubber is slippery so check it out thoroughly before making the investment.

There are many methods of transporting Miniature Horses, you just have to decide what works best for you and what your bank account can handle.

BREEDING MINIATURE HORSES

In Chapter Five I covered how to select breeding quality horses. Hopefully, before beginning a breeding program, you have become knowledgeable about conformation and you now know what separates top quality from mediocrity. (See also Chapter Twelve.) You should also be conversant with the *Standard of Perfection** for the breed and have a clear mental image of the type of horse you wish to breed. In addition, I strongly urge you to acquire a good working knowledge of genetic principles (see Chapter Ten).

Last, and probably one of the most important prerequisites for becoming a successful breeder is the ability to be objective about your horses. The perfect horse has yet to be bred. They all have at least a few faults: mine do and so will yours. You must be aware of the faults within your herd in order to eliminate them. I have never understood why some breeders become so emotionally involved that they become incapable of being objective about their stock. This is very prevalent in the dog show world, and I have seen its equivalent among horse people. You must be able to separate your feelings about your animals where selection of breeding pairs is concerned or you will never achieve your goals in any breeding program in the horse world.

Contact the Registry for a complete description of the Standard of Perfection. Information about Miniature Horse Registries can be found in Chapter Fourteen.

Choosing The Correct Stallion For Your Mare

I'll assume that you do not yet own your own stallion and are now faced with the task of finding the proper mate for your mare.

First, be aware of those faults in your mare you would most like to improve. For instance, if your mare has front feet that toe out, you will look for a stallion whose front feet face dead front. Hopefully he will be proven and you will have seen enough of his foals and their mothers to know if he is dominant genetically for producing straight front legs and feet. If half of his babies toe out and the other half are correct, this stud is not dominant for that trait. Your chances of the foal being true in front are only 50/50. However, if 75% of his get display the desired straight front legs, he is probably a good risk for your mare.

It is incorrect to breed one extreme to another in order to produce the desired quality. In other words, you do not breed a mare who toes out to a stallion who toes in, hoping the foal will be straight. This rarely occurs. More than likely, you will get a foal who either toes in or toes out. The stallion must be correct in the trait you wish to improve in your mare.

After you have decided exactly what needs correction in your mare, keep each trait in mind as you look at stallions. Chances are you will not find a stallion who complements her in every area where she is faulty, so you must know your priorities. Which traits are most important to you to improve first? Make a list in order of importance.

Let us assume you want better front legs, a more refined head, flatter croup, and smaller bone size in your foal. You have found a stallion who is correct in all areas except his head is not as refined as you would like. The majority of his foals are correct for all these traits, but their heads are common, like their sire's. You must decide if you can wait another generation or two to work on the head quality in order to try and improve the other traits. This is an issue that only you, the breeder can decide. Keep in mind that you are not going to achieve your breeding goals within only one or two generations. Establishing a gene pool which breeds true generation after generation can be a life-long endeavor, especially with horses where you must wait three years or more for the next generation.

What if you find a stallion who has all the needed traits but is young and unproven? Try to see his parents, grandparents, sisters, brothers or any close relatives you can. If they too seem to be correct in these same areas, he might be a good risk.

There's an old saying that goes, "Marry not the only fair maid in the clan." This translates into genetics to mean that one outstanding individual in a predominantly mediocre family will not be likely to reproduce his good quality. This also applies in reverse. You may have an average individual who consistently produces quality much greater than his own. Upon further investigation you will almost always find that his close relatives were outstanding individuals who consistently produced outstanding quality.

What if you find a stallion you like but he is unproven and his parents or other close relatives are unknown or unavailable for viewing? You pay your money and you take your chance's. Maybe you will get lucky and have a beautiful foal and maybe you won't. This individual is a true risk.

Aside from conformation, which was covered in Chapter Five, what traits should be avoided in a stallion? .

Poor temperament is not a common problem with Miniatures, but to make certain it never will be, do not breed to a stallion whose temperament is questionable. Make sure both testicles have descended. Do not breed to a stallion who has consistently produced dwarves and be sure to check for correct bite.

The Breeding Contract

You have found the stallion to whom you wish to breed your mare. What can you expect to get for your stud fee besides live sperm?

Almost all established breeders and stud farms dealing with standard size horses have routine contracts and procedures they employ with each mare bred. Breeding is a business and should be run as such. A written contract protects both parties. You should know exactly what guarantees you are getting and what is included for your stud fee.

Each stallion owner has the right to establish his own stud fee and guarantees. Almost all will guarantee a live foal who will stand and nurse. Should the foal die after the first 24 hours of life, the stud owner rarely claims responsibility.

Some stallion owners will guarantee color in the case of pintos or appaloosas.

You should know what the daily cost of mare care will be. You are responsible for any Vet or farrier (horse shoer/trimmer) bills for your mare.

You should know who is liable should either the mare or the stallion be injured by the other. What if your mare dies before she foals? Can you breed another mare back to the stallion? What if your mare dies while staying at the stud farm?

It does not matter whether the stallion owner is your best friend or a complete stranger, you should put your agreement down in writing. It could prevent some real problems later. Try to cover every eventuality, that way you are both protected.

Preparing Your Mare For Breeding

Assume your mare has been on a steady vaccination and worming schedule. Double check to be sure she is up to date on everything. Hopefully, she is in good weight and physical condition.

It is helpful to have a record of her estrus cycle, but this can sometimes be difficult. Some mares will not show obvious signs of heat unless there is a stallion around. Signs to watch for are: frequent urination in small amounts, holding the tail up and 'winking' of the vulva, squatting and raising the tail (usually under the nose of another horse). Being able to present the stud owner with a record will be helpful, but is not imperative.

The stallion owner may want a uterine culture of your mare, especially if she has had a history of pregnancy or conception problems. This also protects the stud. This is done by a Veterinarian while the mare is in estrus. If the culture shows an active infection, medication can be given before breeding to prevent further problems. Either your Vet or the stallion owner's Vet can do this check.

You and the owner of the stallion should decide when your mare will be delivered for breeding. If the stallion lives far away or in a different climate, you would be wise to deliver the mare as early in the year as possible. This will give her a chance to acclimatize to her new environment before breeding. Sometimes a change can cause delay or even cessation of estrus for a short period.

It is usually wise to leave your mare at the stud farm until she is considered to be in foal. Most mares show an estrus cycle every 21 days. If from the time she is bred until 45 days later she has shown no sign of heat when being regularly teased by the stallion, it is probably safe to consider her to be in foal.

Early Pregnancy Detection

Early pregnancy detection in Miniature Horses is difficult. Because they are so small, rectal palpation of the uterus is not possible unless your Veterinarian has a very small hand. In addition, this sometimes requires a tranquilizer. Given in small amounts, this might not be harmful to an established pregnancy, but I personally am always a bit leery of giving any kind of medication to a pregnant animal.

Blood tests are the method I use with my mares to confirm pregnancy. A sample of blood must be taken between 55 and 120 days of gestation for one type of blood test. A positive result is 95% accurate, but a negative does not always mean no pregnancy exists. Another test is accurate as early as 18 days after gestation.

There are also some new ultrasound machines on the market which are supposedly very accurate for Miniatures. In my opinion these hold the most promise for the Miniature Horse breeder. More and more Vets are using them with 100% accuracy and safety. They not only tell if the mare is pregnant; the Vet can tell what day of gestation the mare is in, and a picture of the fetus appears on a video monitor. Some machines even include an instant camera so a photo can be taken!

Breeding chute with kick guard

Mare, with tail wrapped, awaits stallion in chute

With the studies underway at this time, it probably will not be too long until there is a safe, reliable test to determine early pregnancy in our little mares. In the mean time I suggest following the advice of your Vet.

Standing Your Own Stallion

If you own your own stallion and have mare owners pestering you to breed their mares to him, you will be adding a whole new dimension to your breeding operation.

Before you make a decision to allow your stallion to stand at public stud, consider that you may someday be faced with the necessity to refuse service to an inferior mare. This is a very difficult thing to do. You do not want to hurt the owners feelings and must learn to be very tactful in voicing a refusal.

There are some very good reasons for turning down an inferior mare. First of all, no breed needs more poor quality animals. The aim is to constantly upgrade the quality, not just produce large numbers of horses. Secondly, guess which parent inevitably gets the blame for the poor quality offspring? The stallion, of course. Don't ask why, I have yet to figure it out. Perhaps because the stallion is more visible to the public eye. The last thing you need when first establishing your stallion's reputation as a prepotent producer of top quality stock is a mediocre foal crop trotting around. You must be selective and breed only those mares worthy of reproducing. Do not use the excuse that the mare will be bred anyway and you might as well be the one to collect the stud fee. She probably will be bred anyway, but is loss of your stallion's reputation worth the loss of a few hundred dollars?

Occasionally you may be presented with a mare for whom your particular stallion is not the best mate. Maybe one or two of her faults are the same as your stud's, and you know of another stallion who is correct in those traits and consistently produces soundness in those areas. If you are wise, you will suggest to the mare's owner that the mare be bred to the other stallion. Once again, your stallion's reputation has nothing to gain from producing faulty foals. A truly dedicated breeder has the breed as a whole in mind.

As a stallion owner, you must have adequate facilities for housing outside mares during the breeding season. This means separate pens with shelters, box stalls, or a pasture arrangement. Do not get greedy and overcrowd or you will be buying trouble.

Regardless of which of the following breeding methods you choose to use, you should always have some arrangement to tease the mare before breeding. This is both for your own mare or an outside mare. A mare who is not in a receptive stage of estrus can injure the stallion in her attempts to escape, while a determined stud can cause grave injury to the mare in his attempts to breed her.

The best arrangement for teasing is to place a strong unclimbable barrier between the pair to be bred. It allows the stallion to sniff the mare while protecting both. If the mare seems receptive to breeding, an actual breeding can be attempted. If she is obviously not ready, tease her each day until she is. Usually once a stallion and mare have bred it is safe to leave them together but not always. Use your good judgement here.

Decide which method you want to use for breeding. Keeping a group of mares with the stallion in a pasture and allowing the horses to breed at will has the advantage of taking less time and work on your part. Also, many breeders feel that the horses know best the most opportune time for breeding and feel that pregnancy frequency increases with this method.

Its disadvantage is that not only does it add to the difficulty of determining if a mare has stopped her estrus cycles, but most probably you will have no idea of the exact due date. You may not even know if the mare has truly been bred. Do be sure your pasture size is large enough for a mare to escape a persistent stallion should she so desire.

Putting one mare in a small pen with the stallion where you can keep an eye on them has all the advantages of the above with fewer disadvantages. Since the pair is confined where you can keep a closer eye on them you can be more aware if breeding takes place and when. The same is true of estrus dates. If they are left together for any length of time, you still will not know exactly when to expect the foal. Before putting a mare and stallion together in the same enclosure, make sure they will get along. You do not need injuries to contend with.

The other method is controlled breeding. The mare is either held with a halter and lead by a handler while standing free or is placed in a breeding chute.

Stallion mounts mare

Stallion completes breeding mare

A breeding chute is a three sided affair which has enough room for the mare to stand, but is narrow enough to keep her from swinging her rear end from side to side. The stallion is then led up to the mare and allowed to mount and breed her. The mare is usually bred every other day from the first day she will accept the stallion until she shows by her actions that she is out of heat.

Using this method you are certain of the breeding dates and thus have a better idea of when to expect the foal. You also have more ability to prevent injuries in the event that either horse gets nasty.

It is helpful to wrap the upper part of the mare's tail to keep it out of the stallions way. Wrap her upper tail in two inch wide masking tape (which works great for this) or you can use a leg bandage.

Some stallions may need manual assistance during breeding. I learned a great deal about the do's and don'ts of helping a stud with my first attempts to breed.

Page is a 4 year old stallion of 30 inches who has sired foals. I have no idea what breeding methods were used with him before I purchased him. The first time I bred him it was to my 29 1/2'' mare. At the first breeding he allowed me to guide his penis to her vagina and a breeding was accomplished.

The next time this was not successful. Every time I would reach for his penis to guide him he would back off the mare. We tried for hours, day after day, using every method we could think of. (His problem was that when he would get an erection his penis lay flat along his belly, and he would either poke the mare at her anus, or project up along her buttocks and over her back!)

I had two friends helping and we tried raising the mare, lowering the mare, turning them loose together in a pen, holding the mare with the stallion loose, holding the stallion with the mare loose, holding both. At one point we were leading the mare at a trot while the stallion was mounted on her in an attempt to lower the angle of the penis! It was a real comedy act but unfunny at the time.

Then I got the bright idea to roll up some cloth shipping boots, wrap them in a sheet secured at both ends like a sausage and tie the whole contraption around Page's belly. The theory was that upon erection the penis would be deflected downward and enter the mare where it was supposed to. Well, not only did this not work, but it had us all convulsed with laughter. Poor little Page, he looked so ridiculous but he tried to breed the mare anyway!

My mare was now out of season but my 14 year old neighbor had a 48'' pony mare she wanted to breed to Page. Since Julie had been such a help to me, I agreed, with the understanding that the baby would not be registered as a Mini. The next question was, if I can't get a breeding to my 29 1/2'' mare, how the devil are we going to breed a 48'' mare to a 30'' stallion who won't allow manual assistance?!?

We first attempted to breed Julie's mare at her place. As instructed by me, Julie had dug a hole for the mare—18 inches straight down and only wide enough for the mare's hind feet to stand in, a bit smaller than I had suggested. The mare was even cooperative enough to put her feet in it! Page, however, was so distracted by the other horses and new surroundings that his penis never even dropped. At this point I decided that a breeding stand was needed.

The next day I built a breeding chute at my place. It was about 5 feet long and 2 feet wide and had a padded kick board at the business end. I then dug the floor out until it gently sloped front to rear to a depth of 15''. Julie brought her mare over and backed her into the chute. When Page mounted her and I reached to guide him I realized why he was backing off. I was holding his penis in my closed hand and pulling it toward the vagina. Realizing that this was probably not pleasant for him, I flattened my hand, palm down and gently pressed him downward until he achieved penetration and a successful breeding. The two subsequent breedings took place in about two minutes as compared to the previous two hours of unsuccessful attempts.

Looking back, I can now laugh about my ineptitude, but there was a real concern about ruining Page as a stud due to my lack of knowledge and experience. I was really fearful that too many unsuccessful breeding tries would reduce his enthusiasm. Perhaps you can learn from my mistakes. Two years after writing this, I was pleasantly surprised by a new baby from a supposedly barren mare and Page. He had learned to breed mares on his own once I left him alone!

If your stallion is unproven it wold be wise to have a sperm count done before using him on your own or outside mares.

There is no advantage in wasting time on a sterile animal or one of low fertility. Your Veterinarian can perform this test for you. Also, ask your Vet's opinion about doing periodic cultures on both mares and stallions. This could prevent an outbreak of infections, an occurrence which all breeding operations can do without.

Extreme size differences can be a problem especially if the stallion is short and the mare is tall. The usual solution is to dig a hole in which the mare's hind legs stand, lowering her rear within easy reach of the stallion (see above!)

STUD FEES

You will need to establish a reasonable stud fee. Check with other stallion owners in your area to determine the average price range. If this will be your stallion's first season at public stud and he has sired no foals as yet, you will probably want to keep his fee low for this first year. Once he has established himself as a consistent producer of good quality foals you can raise his fee. Just be careful not to price him out of the market or you will find him retired much earlier than you had planned!

You should take the time to draw up a breeding contract as discussed in the beginning of this Chapter. You decide what you are willing to guarantee, what responsibilities you will assume for the mares in your care, what services you are going to offer and write it all down. You would probably be wise to spend some extra money and have a lawyer approve the contract before having it printed. You do not want to have a law suit should a mare be injured or die while under your care. If possible, ask some breeders to let you see their contracts which will give you a better idea of how to word everything.

When the mares begin arriving, ask the owners to bring some of their feed, especially if their diet has been radically different from what you feed your own horses. If you feed hay and they feed pellets, have the owner bring enough to switch the mare over to hay during a three to four day period. Also, ask the owner to provide any special vitamin supplement which they may be feeding. The mare will undergo enough stress because of her new surroundings without the added stress of a sudden diet change which could cause digestive upsets.

THE BREEDERS SPEAK:
RESULTS OF A SURVEY

When the first edition was published, I sent questionnaires to sixty-seven Miniature Horse owners and breeders and received 26 responses. The results of that survey are presented here.

1.   What methods do you incorporate to improve your stock?
  — Outcross only: 1
  — Line Breeding: 4
  — Phenotype selection and culling: 9
  — Size only: 1
  — Genotype/Phenotype and experimental inbreeding: 1
  — No Answer: 10

2.   Do you cull your stock?
  — Yes: 22
  — No:
  — No answer: 4

3.   Are you satisfied with the quality you see in the breed today? (I probably should have worded this question better.)
  — Yes: 2
  — No: 11
  — Yes and No: 12
  — No Answer: 1

4.   When you breed a mare, do you try to select a stallion whose conformation is good where hers is faulty?

— Yes: 20
— No Answer: 4

5. Should there be only one Registry in the USA?
— Yes: 20
— No: 1
— No Answer: 5

6. Should certain faults disqualify a Miniature from being shown?
— Yes: 20
— No: 2
— No Answer: 4
— *Which ones:*
— Dwarfism: 11
— Over 34''in height: 6
— Over/undershot mouth: 8
— Monorchids: 5
— Cataracts: 1
— Bad Legs: 3
— Club feet: 1
— Bad Head: 2
— Deformities: 2
Some responses listed several faults, all of which are reported here.

7. Should every Mini have to pass examination and measurement by a Registry representative before being permanently registered?
[Most were in favor of this but also added that to carry it out would be highly impractical and expensive.]
— Yes: 15
— No: 4
— Uncertain: 2
— No Answer: 5

8. Should dwarves be registered?
— Yes: 1
— No: 19
— Uncertain: 2
— No Answer: 4

9. Are the Mini's referred to as being a specific "breed", such as Arabs, truly bred down from Arabs: or are they simply a different "type" of Mini cropping up within the breed?
— Different type: 2
— Bred Down: 16
— Uncertain: 2
— No Answer: 6

10. Do you ever use pony breed crosses within your breeding program?
[Those who responded with a "Yes" were trying to incorporate traits into Miniatures which were difficult to find in the majority of Mini's.]
— Yes: 6
— No: 15
— No Answer: 5

11. Can a buyer tell if there is pony blood in stock he is thinking of buying?
— Yes: 4
— No: 9
— Uncertain: 5
— No Answer: 8

12. Is the Miniature Horse a good monetary investment and can breeding them provide a good income?
— Yes: 15
— No: 1
— Uncertain: 9
— No Answer: 1

13. Do you feel a buyer should have a horse Vet-checked before purchase?
— Yes: 13
— No: 3
— Sometimes: 5
— No Answer: 5

14. What information, guarantees, etc., should be included in a sales contract?
— Stallions to have both testicles descended by three years of age: 2

— Pregnant mares re-bred if not pregnant: 4
— Free breeding for mares: 1
— True pedigree: 4
— Size of parents: 2
— Health: 10
— Size guarantee in horses under three years old: 7
— Proof of Registration: 4
— Foaling record in non-maiden mares: 2
— No guarantees should be given: 1
— No Answer: 4

15. Do you take a continued interest in the horse and make yourself available to help the buyer after the sale is concluded?
— Yes: 22
— No:
— No Answer: 4

16. What type of fencing do you recommend for a Mini?
— V-mesh: 1
— Woven Wire: 8
— Chain Link: 6
— Wire mesh and wood used together: 2
— Board: 3
— "Safe" fencing: 3
— No Answer: 2

17. What is the minimum size for a box stall?
Range was 6' by 6' to 10' by 20'. Average size was 8' by 8'.
— No Answer: 5

18. Do you feed vitamins? How do you scale down the amount from that recommended for standard horses?
— Yes: 14
— No: 8
— 1/8 Normal dose: 1
— 1/10th: 1
— 1/4th: 3
— 1/2: 2
— Ask Vet: 5
— By weight of Horse: 2

19.   Do you think a child should be allowed to ride a Mini? If so, what is the top weight you would recommend?
— Yes: 17
— No: 3
— No Answer: 6
(Those who answered in the affirmative mostly indicated a mature 34" horse and a top weight for the rider of 60 pounds.)

20.   What advice would you give to a novice who is purchasing their foundation stock:

A. Should they buy a stallion if they only have one or 2 mares?
— Yes: 4
— No: 16
— No Answer: 6
Most "No" responses qualified this by stating 'as long as a good quality stallion is available to breed to.

B. What is the best size for a brood mare?
— 30" : 1
— 30" - 32": 2
— 31" - 32": 3
— 31" - 34": 2
— 32" - 33": 2
— 32" - 34": 4
— 34"   : 1
— No Answer: 11

C. How young can a mare be when she is first bred?
— 1 Year: 1
— 2 Years: 12
— Long two year old: 2
— 3 Years: 7
— No Answer: 4

D. What are the most important points in conformation that a brood mare should have?
— Good Head: 7
— Good Legs: 9
— Good Feet: 2
— Good Bite: 2

— Good Tail Set: 1
— Good Body: 3
— Good Movement: 1
— Good Proportion: 8
— Good Temperament: 1
— Well Sprung Ribs: 2
— Broad Pelvis: 2
— Vulva Not Protruding Beyond Anus: 1
— No Answer: 8

E. What serious faults should be avoided?
— Poor Head: 5
— Long Body: 3
— Short Neck: 1
— Steep Croup: 1
— Poor Legs: 9
— Bad Feet: 1
— Bad Bite: 9
— Genetic History of Dwarfism: 1
— Dwarf Traits: 5
— Wasp Waist: 1
— Roached Back: 1
— Narrow Body: 1
— Poor Temperament: 1
— No Answer: 7

21. Will you breed to an oversize mare?
— Yes: 13
— No: 7
— No Answer: 6

22. Have you found any reliable method for determining early pregnancy? What is it and how accurate is it?
— Yes: 6
— No: 15
— No Answer: 5
Blood test between 45-120 days gestation—95% accurate. Ultrasound testing—100% accurate. Teasing with stallion—no percentage given. Manual check—no percentage given.

23. Do you feel that Miniature Horse's have special problems foaling?
— Yes: 9

— No: 13
— No Answer: 4

24. Dwarfism: Keep in mind that there are degrees of Dwarfism—each animal is different and must be dealt with on an individual basis. The wording of my questions was too general.

A. Should dwarves be humanely put to sleep?
— Yes: 12
— No: 6
— No Answer: 8

B. Can they function as normal horses?
— Yes: 10
— No: 4
— No Answer: 12
(Apparently some can and some cannot)

C. Are they in pain?
— Yes: 4
— No: 15
— No Answer: 7
(Some are and some are not)

D. Do you feel that Dwarves should be seen by the public?
— Yes: 3
— No: 17
— No Answer: 6

25. Do you have a working knowledge of applied Genetics?
— Yes: 15
— No: 6
— No Answer: 9

26. Do you use genetic considerations within your breeding program?
— Yes: 16
— No: 1
— No Answer: 9

27. Do you follow any particular genetic method such as linebreeding or inbreeding within your program?
— Yes: 16

— No: 5
— No Answer: 5

28. What do you think are the most serious problems within the breed today?
— Poor Legs: 4
— Steep Croup: 1
— Inaccurate Pedigrees: 2
— Size is being reduced too fast: 3
— Dwarfism: 2
— Bad Bites: 4
— Use of Oversize Stock: 1
— Size too big: 1
— Poor Heads: 2
— Foaling and Infertility: 1
— Breeders: 2
— No Answer: 11

29. Can a mare be too small to breed?
— Yes: 17
— No: 2
— No Answer: 7
(One Breeder stated that length and breadth of body was more important than height.)

30. Do you think quality and soundness have been sacrificed in the quest for smaller size?
— Yes: 16
— No: 3
— No Answer: 7

By now it must be apparent that there are many divergent opinions and beliefs among those who breed Miniature Horses. The above list was not printed as a guide for the beginner, but more as evidence that there really is no single *correct* method which must be followed verbatim. You, as a future breeder or exhibitor, must learn and use the methods which work best for you and your horses.

GENETICS—BASIS OF ALL INHERITANCE

Let me state here and now that I am not a geneticist nor do I claim to be an expert on this subject. I have, however, done a great deal of reading on the subject of genetics and have used and studied it in my many years of breeding Great Danes, birds and horses.

Once the basic principles are learned and understood, it becomes an invaluable tool. In addition to using it to breed improvement, it helps you to understand why certain traits that were not seen in the conformation of the parents can turn up in the foal's conformation. You no longer feel as if you are groping blindly in the dark in your quest to improve your horses.

I do not intend to delve too deeply into how the sperm and ovum carry the genes, nor into too many of the mechanics of microscopic reproduction. This subject can be learned from many good texts written for the layman in comprehensible terms. If you have little or no knowledge of these basic facts, you should first learn your basics as it will give you a better understanding of the information contained in this chapter.

I have included my own basic descriptions and without some knowledge of reproduction, you will not understand the concepts in this chapter. Mainly I intend to explain how genetic understanding can be used to accomplish your breeding goals and how I use it. You can also use the information to guide your purchases of Mini's.

The Importance of a Pedigree

In assembling a group of animals to use for breeding, the more information you have about each animals' relatives, the more accurately you can predict what traits that particular animal is likely to pass on to its offspring. The ancestral names which appear on a pedigree have no value unless you have specific information about as many individuals as possible. In the case of Miniature Horses it is sometimes difficult to see the parents, not to mention the grandparents. Often the parents are listed as unknown. When this is the case you are breeding blind and have no indication of what your horse will produce. So what about the saying, "like begets like"? Often it is true but occasionally it is not. That is why genetic study is helpful. The individual animal is a product of his parent's genetic make-up.

The Mechanics of Inheritance

Some elementary genetic principles must be illustrated here in order to understand what follows.

The new foal inherits half his genes from his sire and half from his dam. The genes are the chemical blueprint which determines every physical characteristic the foal will have. They determine his size, color, temperament, length of mane and tail, whether his legs are straight or crooked, whether his head is pretty or common, on and on for every part of his body inside and out.

There are two types of cells in the horse, as in other living organisms. The body cells, known as **SOMATIC** cells are found in all tissues of the body such as skin, internal organs, bone, etcetera. The other type of cells are the sex cells, called **GAMATES**. These are the sperm cells in the stallion and the egg cells, or ova, in the mare.

The gamates carry only **ONE HALF** the chromosomes of the somatic cells. Since the genes are contained within the chromosomes, this means that the gamates only have one half of the genes of the body cells. This seems to be the most difficult concept for the beginning student of genetic inheritance to grasp so I have included the following illustrations to help clarify this point.

The following illustration, is a **SOMATIC CELL** (body cell). It contains the nucleus which contains the 64 pairs of chromosomes, which contain the genes. (Only three pairs are shown for the sake of clarity).

Illustration #1

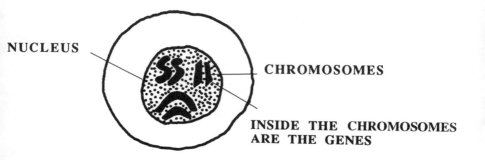

NUCLEUS

CHROMOSOMES

INSIDE THE CHROMOSOMES ARE THE GENES

Somatic Cell (Body Cell)—Contains nucleus which contains the 64 pairs of chromosomes which contain the genes.

Illustration #2

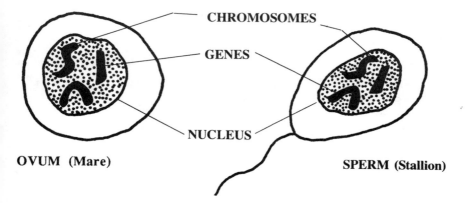

CHROMOSOMES

GENES

NUCLEUS

OVUM (Mare)

SPERM (Stallion)

The gamates (sex cells), when manufactured within the testes and ovaries, have only 32 chromosomes. The 64 pairs of chromosomes have split, each half carrying their respective genes.

93

Illustration #3

FERTILIZED OVUM

CHROMOSOMES ARE ONCE AGAIN PAIRED

When the ovum is fertilized by the sperm, each carrying only one half of each parents genetic material, the new embryo has the full compliment of 64 chromosomes or 32 *pairs* of chromosomes with their genes. This foal is a unique individual whose total genetic make-up is unlike any other.

Dominant and Recessive Genes

Without going into deep technical detail it is important to understand the basic concept of dominant and recessive genes. Since these types of genes exist (along with modifiers, masking genes, and incomplete dominants which will not be discussed here in any detail) there occurs a phenomenon whereby an individual may carry genes to express a specific trait (genotype) but the trait is not expressed physically (phenotype).

Let me be more specific. *Genotype* means the sum total of a particular individual's genetic makeup. *Phenotype* is the visible and measurable expression of those genes—or what you actually can see of the animal's conformation, color etc. You are now confused and wondering why the two are different. After all, if an individual carries genes which affect a specific trait, such as his color, surely he will be that color, right? Not always, and here is why you need to know about dominant and recessive genes.

I will use coat color pattern as an example since it is an easy trait to see and understand. The gene which produces the tobiano spotting pattern in horses is a *dominant* gene. The gene which produces a solid colored coat, allowing the pigment to cover the largest

94

portion of the body is *recessive* to the tobiano gene. (Do not get confused here because I've not mentioned a specific color such as black or chestnut, etc. The solid color gene only affects the placement of the color: i.e., *solid* black or *solid* chestnut). Since tobiano *spotting* is the dominant gene, a horse showing this spotting pattern as his phenotype can still carry the solid color gene recessively as part of his genotype. Remember I stated that each parent carries two sets of genes and chromosomes but gives the offspring only half their chromosomes, thus half their genes.

Solid color coat is produced by a gene that is recessive.

Tobiano color pattern (spotting) is produced by a dominant gene for coat color.

Illustration #4

Sperm, carrying their respective genes, engaged in the great race!

Illustration #5

The solid mare donates one of her two recessive solid genes, the tobiano stallion donates one of his dominate tobiano genes. Their offspring carries one gene for each color pattern as his genotype but his phenotype can *never be solid because the tobiano gene is the dominant one of the pair.*

Now we have a whole new ball game. What happens if this new individual who carries both a tobiano and solid pattern gene (making him genetically heterozygous* for solid AND tobiano) is mated to a mare who is genotypically identical to him, meaning she carries the same genetic makeup for solid and tobiano patterns being phenotypically tobiano.

*If he was pure for tobiano as was his sire, having no solid gene, he would be homozygous, meaning he carries *only* genes for tobiano.

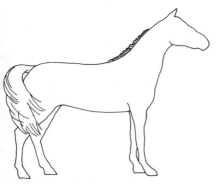

Solid Mare (ss)
Genotype Homozygous for solid
Phenotype -- solid

Tobiano Stallion (TT)
Genotype Homozygous for tobiano
Phenotype -- tobiano spotted

Offspring

Tobiano spotted foal (Ts)
Genotype heterozygous for tobiano and soli‹
Phenotype -- tobiano

There is no certain way to predict exactly how the genes will combine unless you are dealing only with animals who are homozygous for the pure dominant or recessive trait. In other words, a mating between a tobiano stallion and tobiano mare-both of whom are homozygous for the tobiano pattern gene, can produce nothing but tobiano offspring all of whom are genotypically homozygous for tobiano *and* all of whom are phenotypically tobiano. A horse which is homozygous for such a trait is said to "breed true" for that trait. (If you are getting confused here, be sure you understand the meaning of homozygous, heterozygous, genotype and phenotype).

The T-S Square

Illustration (#6) shows the color expectancy from the above proposed mating of the heterozygous tobiano spotted horses. Let T represent the dominant tobiano gene and s represent the recessive solid gene. This is based on repeating the breeding four times giving four offspring.

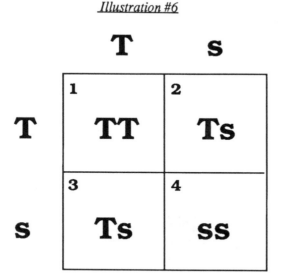

Illustration #6

Each square represents one foal and it's genotype and phenotype for the tobiano and solid genes.

Square #1

This foal's genotype (TT) contains two genes for tobiano. His coat pattern is tobiano. He can pass on *only* tobiano genes to his offspring since he is homozygous for the tobiano gene and does not carry a solid pattern gene recessively.

Squares #2 and #3

These foals' genotypes (Ts) each contain one gene for tobiano and one for solid. Their coat patterns are tobiano. They can pass on either the tobiano or the solid gene to their offspring since they are heterozygous for tobiano and solid. Since the solid gene is recessive to tobiano, it is not able to express itself in the foals' phenotypes.

Square #4

This foal is our example of two recessive genes finding each other and expressing a genetic trait of the parents which the parents did not show in their phenotype. This foal's genotype (ss) contains two genes for solid color pattern. His coat color pattern is solid. He can only pass on solid genes to his offspring since he is homozygous for solid. If he carried a tobiano gene, he would *appear* tobiano since tobiano is dominant to solid.

The chart is a shorthand method of calculating the probability of any two genes finding each other at the moment of conception. The heterozygous male has sperm which carry a solid gene and a tobiano gene. The heterozygous mare has ova with the same makeup: half carry the solid gene and half carry the tobiano. It is pure chance which sperm finds which egg. The laws of probability tell us however that in a sampling of 100 offspring, approximately 25% will be TT, 25% will be ss, and 50% will be Ts, as illustrated in #6.

If you have already grasped the concept, please bear with me as I give one more example. It is imperative that these principles be understood since they are the very foundation of genetics. The next graph (Illustration #7) mates a tobiano stallion with a heterozygous genotype for solid and tobiano (Ts), to a solid mare. Homozygous for the solid color pattern (ss).

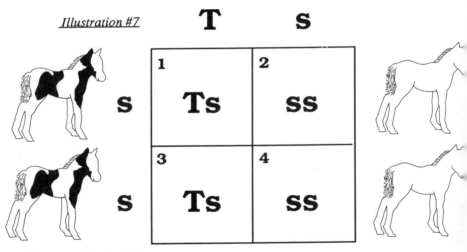

Illustration #7

Squares #1 & #3
Both foals have tobiano phenotypes and heterozygous genotypes for solid and tobiano.

Both can pass on either solid or tobiano genes to their offspring.

Squares #2 & #4
These foals have solid phenotypes and genotypes since a double dose of a recessive genotype is necessary for the type to find expression. If they are bred to a solid mate they will produce nothing but solid coat patterns.

I have taken you through all the above in order to more clearly explain the behavior of simple dominant and recessive gene pairs. since the chromosomes occur in pairs in the somatic cells, so do genes. I'm going to continue with the example of the solid color gene versus the tobiano spotting gene.

As we said before, these traits are controlled by single genes (not multigenetic as are most traits) and tobiano is dominant over solid color.

As previously stated, when gamates, (sex cells), are formed, they contain only half of the genetic make-up of each parent. One gamate may end up with the gene which causes tobiano spotting and the other gamate may carry another gene for solid body color.

It is pure chance as to which of the mare's ova becomes ripe first and ovulates into the uterus to await the stallion's sperm.

The same holds true of the stallion's sperm. Approximately one-half of the millions of sperm contained in each ejaculation carry his solid color gene and one half carry the tobiano gene.

The laws of probability tell us that with animals carrying simple recessives and simple dominants, the chances are always 50-50 as to which gene is inherited by the foal. The calculations are based on 100 offspring. So, if your tobiano stallion has been bred to 15 solid pattern mares and has produced 15 solid foals, there is **STILL** a 50-50 chance that the next foal he sires will be spotted. This also tells you something about his genotype. You **know** he carries a recessive gene for solid because he has produced solid foals even though he is himself tobiano. You also know that he carries the dominant tobiano gene because he **is** tobiano.

Sometimes semantics seems to be responsible for some mis-understandings. One breeder once asked me why her tobiano stallion didn't always produce spotted foals if the tobiano gene was domi-nant. She didn't understand that the gene *had to be passed along* in order for it to be able to exert it's dominance. The chances of the tobiano gene being passed along, when the horse carries a recessive gene for solid as well, are 50-50. Only horses who are homozygous for the tobiano gene (they have two genes for tobiano and carry *no* gene for solid) will produce 100% tobiano foals.

Admittedly the above examples are, perhaps, overly simple when compared to multigenetically controlled traits. There are other types of genes which behave in different ways. In order to accurately predict expectancy of certain traits you must have a pretty good idea of the correct information on the ancestors.

The example of equine coat color can be translated to explain many traits of Miniature Horses. Tobiano is dominant to solid, but there is a recessive gene for another type of spotting called *overo* which seems to be recessive to both solid and tobiano. (The genetic make-up of the overo pattern is still not completely understood).

The relationship between genes: which is dominant and which are recessive, can be likened to a pecking order among chickens. The rooster (most dominant gene) is at the top of the heap and bosses everyone around. Next is the bossiest hen who only takes orders from the rooster. Below her are the rank and file of her subordinates, all of whom listen to their betters, and in turn, control their underlings until you come to the bottom of the heap and find the little hen (most recessive gene) whom everyone picks on. She never gets to eat or express herself until she is the only one in the barnyard.

Now you are beginning to wonder how any of this can be helpful since little is known of the mode of inheritance of most equine traits. Also, few traits are controlled by a single gene. Most are multigenetic.

Head Shape

There are probably thousands of genes and their modifiers which make up the blueprint to determine the shape of a horse's head. Although it is close to impossible (not to mention impractical) to try isolating each gene and how it behaves in creating the overall blueprint, the controlling groups of genes often tend to act in recessive or dominant ways.

Let us say you have a stallion with a beautiful Arab-type head. You mate him to ten mares whose head types range from ugly to plain, but none are beautiful. If 75% of the offspring have beautiful heads like their sire, you can be fairly accurate in concluding that your stallion is dominant for his head type. This can be applied to any conformation trail or group of traits which tend to occur in the same manner.

But what about traits which, as a group, behave in a recessive manner? Since recessives are masked by dominants, they can be difficult to isolate. The recessive genes usually control undesirable traits such as an undershot jaw or monkey bite. This is when the lower teeth protrude in front of the upper teeth causing all kinds of problems which will be discussed later. (See Photos in Chapter 12.)

We will use an undershot bite as our example. Assume you breed a mare and stallion to each other who both possess a correct bite. Their foal has an undershot jaw. What does this tell us? It is highly probable that *both* parents are carriers of the recessive gene or genes which produced the bad bite. What makes a trait like this difficult to breed out is its recessive nature. The foal could as easily have had a correct bite and still carried the genes for a bad bite recessively. These recessives can be masked by their dominant alleles (genes which appear on a common location on the chromosomes) for generation after generation until the time when they pair with another like recessive and express themselves in the horse's phenotype. If you will refer back, once again, to Illustration #6, you will see that there is a 50% probability that an offspring of recessive carrier parents will itself be a carrier.

This is a rather sobering thought, especially when one realizes that in dealing with horses, test breeding to identify carriers of recessive genetic defects is a life-long project. Since a mare can only produce one offspring yearly, obtaining the number of animals needed for a definitive test can take years and years. Testing a stallion is a more feasible alternative, but once again, you are going to tie up your valuable breeding mares as test subjects even *if*, they are qualified in the traits for which you are testing. Few breeders can afford to purchase and maintain a separate herd of mares whose only function is to test the genetic makeup of the stallion.

So what is the logical solution to this problem? The solution: intelligent breedign practices and ruthless culling. These will be discussed in Chapter 12.

Breeding Methods

Inbreeding

Inbreeding is generally considered to be the closest type of breeding possible. It includes breeding full brother to full sister, mother to son, and father to daughter. Ironically, sister to brother matings may not be genetically close at all since the possibility exists for each sibling to receive entirely different sets of genes from each parent. This is however, seldom the case, and we can assume it to be inbreeding for our purposes.

Those who do not understand genetic principles often condemn inbreeding, claiming that it weakens the animal which it produces. In many cases this can be true, but inbreeding itself is not the culprit.

By its very nature inbreeding allows the greatest probability that recessive genes will be expressed (show up). This is because closely related animals are more likely to carry the same recessives in their genotype than unrelated animals. By breeding these close relatives to each other the chances are high that two recessive genes or groups or recessive genes will pair and produce the trait they control in the animal's phenotype.

What can be observed is that the recessive trait is often undesirable, such as dwarfism or an incorrect mouth. If the trait the pair control is desirable, then inbreeding is considered to be successful, but you often get a little of each.

Inbreeding can be a very useful tool for pinpointing an animal's genotype. When inbreeding is employed in horses, it is safest after linebreeding has set a type, and you have a related herd of animals who consistently produce the qualities you have been striving to "set" in your breeding line.

You should have a very clear idea of what your gene pool is capable of producing and then use only animals whose phenotype is as nearly perfect as possible. Even then it can be risky, but if successful, you have a real prize. It is definitely not for the novice breeder.

Linebreeding
This practice usually includes pairings such as: niece to uncle, grandchild to grandparent, half sister to half brother, or a pedigree which includes one animal's name somewhere within the first three generations on *both* sides of the pedigree. Linebreeding is probably the safest approach when establishing a breeding herd. Although recessives can certainly be expressed when using this method, the frequency is not as high as with inbreeding. There is a wider margin for error here because progress is more gradual.

As mentioned previously, it is often not easy to procure Miniature Horses from ancestry where the close relatives beyond the parents can be seen. When this is the case, linebreeding in the beginning of a breeding program becomes close to impossible. If half-brothers and half-sisters are available, this system then becomes feasible. Just keep in mind that the individuals to be mated must both be good specimens and not have faults in common.

Outcrossing

This is the mating of unrelated animals. Unlike inbreeding and linebreeding this method will do nothing to make the resulting foal more homozygous genetically. It is very difficult to predict with any accuracy what results might be obtained from such a mating. The continued use of this breeding method will never produce a group of animals which breed true for any characteristic.

One advantage of this method is that you are less likely to encounter any recessive genetic problems unless, unknowingly, two animals are crossed which both carry one of these in their genotype.

Outcrossing can best be used when, after several generations of linebreeding you have established a gene pool which breeds true most of the time for the traits you desire, but you find that your gene pool does not contain genes for producing, for example, a beautiful head.

What do you do? The time has come to outcross. Your best bet for finding the right animal to whom to outcross is to locate an animal from a *linebred* family with outstanding heads, who consistently produces foals with outstanding heads. Even though this animal himself is the result of linebreeding, he is unrelated to your own animals, and the resultant breeding is considered an outcross. Then you take the good-headed result of this mating and breed it back to one from your own linebred herd. You have now gained the genes you need to work with in order to put better head type on your future horses.

Besides the above outlined breeding techniques, there are several others. I will not go into them here but many breeding books can fully explain them to you. Much can be learned from books concerned with breeding other types of animals such as dogs, cattle, chickens, etc.

FOALING

If you do not believe that two months can seem as long as two centuries, just wait until your mare has only eight weeks until her due date! Never will time move so slowly as it does during this endless vigil.

Gestation

The duration of gestation can range from 300 days to 400 days with the norm being 340 days or a few days past eleven months. One breeder who keeps meticulous records stated that her Mini's average gestation period is from 325 to 330 days.

Before your mare's last month, collect the following supplies in a place convenient to where she will foal: seven percent iodine solution, a cup or container wide enough to immerse the umbilical stump (this will prevent infection from entering the foal via the umbilical cord), clean terry cloth towels (these are to clean the mucous from the foal's nostrils and mouth, and are also used to help dry the foal), a bucket of clean water to store the placenta until the Vet can ascertain that it is whole and no part has been left in the mare to cause infection, a Fleet Enema in case the foal has trouble passing the meconium, bran for a warm mash for your mare after she has foaled.

If your foaling area lacks light, have a functioning flashlight available. Keep your Veterinarian's phone number by the phone in case of an emergency.

Prior to foaling decide where you want your mare to foal. In good weather, an easily accessible, grassy pasture is ideal, especially if you can arrange to be nearby to keep watch. The cleaner the area, the better. The next best choice in good weather is a large corral bedded with clean straw.

If your mare is going to need to be in a box stall due to bad weather, make sure it's at least 10' by 10' and bedded in straw. Shavings or sawdust can cause respiration problems in a new born foal and is not usually recommended.

Some breeders, myself included, have installed a closed circuit TV in the foaling stall at the barn with a monitor screen in the house. This has worked very well, especially on cold rainy nights when the thought of trudging out to the barn every two hours is enough to make one wonder if sanity has fled!

Another mare monitor I will never again be without is a "Baby Buzzer". The "Baby Buzzer", and similar monitors are advertised in the various breed journals. This device consists of a detector/transmitter which the mare wears on a special circle ring. When she lays flat on her side, in foaling position, the transmitter sends a signal to a remote receiver which emits a high-pitched buzz.

This receiver can be wired to a second receiver which can be placed several hundred feet away from the mare, such as the bedroom. When the signal goes off, it wakes me. All I have to do is open my eyes and look at the closed circuit TV. If it is a false alarm, I go back to sleep. If not, I'm off to the barn. Although these sets are not cheap, I recommend them highly. They are worth every penny! If you save the life of only one foal or mare, they have paid for themselves.

Do whatever works best for you, but do plan to keep a very sharp eye on your mare so you can help her if she gets into trouble. It is not uncommon for the newborn foal to be unable to break the sack and suffocate. This is a simple chore for you if you are there at the birth.

Most mares will begin to show some enlargement of the udder a month or so before foaling. A week prior to foaling a yellowish, waxy secretion will sometimes appear at the ends of the teats. Sometimes milk can be seen dripping from the teats. If the mare drips a lot of milk be sure the foal is either given frozen colostrum from another mare or that you have your Veterinarian check her antibody titer for immunities.

It is not unusual for the uterus to contract irregularly from time to time as parturition approaches, sometimes a couple weeks prior to birth. At these times the mare may become restless, stamp her feet, look at her belly and generally show signs of being colicky. There is usually much tail swishing. This is normal and you should not be concerned.

As foaling time nears, the fetus is turned into birth position and you will often see a depression or softening of the muscles on either side of the mare's croup just above the tail bone. The vulva will enlarge and relax. A mucous discharge from the vulva will often be seen. She may walk with difficulty usually seen as straddling of the rear legs. Manure and urine voiding become frequent and quantities smaller.

Just prior to birth, the mare will often, but not always refuse her food. As the contractions become stronger, she becomes restless. She may bite at her sides, sweat, swish her tail, lie down, get up, roll, rub her body against a wall or fence, and give every indication of having a severe case of colic. The water bag makes its appearance through the vulva and often breaks. The mare will usually lie down at this point.

After a few violent contractions, the foal's forefeet appear, one slightly ahead of the other, still encased in the membrane. At this point check to make sure the bottoms of the feet are facing *down*. If they are not, call your Veterinarian *immediately*!! The foal is up-side down, or breach, and must be turned before it can be born. Do not attempt this yourself as you can cause injury to the mare and the foal. The Vet may want you to get the mare on her feet and start her walking to help alleviate the intensity of the contractions until he can get to you. Ask him what to do until he arrives.

If feet are pointing down as they should and the nose lies on the forelegs, all is well and you may relax. A couple more strong contractions and the baby is born. If the mare is laboring hard and the foal is positioned correctly, and after a few minutes no progress is being made, you can assist the mare. Break the sack and grasp the forelegs with a towel. When the mare has a contraction, a steady downward arc-pull (towards the mare's hocks) may be exerted. This will usually ease the delivery, especially for a maiden mare. If hard

111

labor continues longer than 30 minutes with no apparent progress, call the Veterinarian.

It is normal for both mare and foal to lie quietly and to rest after their ordeal. If the foal's head is still encased in the membrane, pull it away (you may need to grasp it with the towel as it is tough and very slippery). Clean the mucous from the nostrils and mouth with a towel. Often the foal's hind feet will still rest within the mare. Within about a half hour, the foal or mare, or both, will try to get to their feet. The umbilicus will break naturally at this time. Do not attempt to make either horse rise or break the cord as the foal is still receiving its blood from the placenta. Approach the mare very quietly so she does not startle and jump to her feet prematurely.

As soon as the cord breaks, immerse the foal's stump in the iodine solution for at least 30 seconds. When the foal tries to stand, do not assist him. He will be awkward and may fall several times before he makes it all the way up. If after two hours he has still not risen or made an attempt to stand, there is probably something wrong and you had better call the Vet.

Even though you may be fully prepared for the coming birth, including the set up closed circuit TV, it is still entirely possible to miss the whole thing as I did! I set my alarm to awaken me every hour so I could look at the screen by my bed. At one point I squinted blindly at the screen and saw what appeared to be a huge spider wobbling across the lens. I started to return to sleep when I realized that what I had seen was certainly no spider! My mare had been her usual sneaky self and foaled with her only sign being her filled udder. Luckily the colt was fine and there were no complications but you really have to be vigilant. (This was before I bought my "Baby Buzzer".)

Once the mare and foal are on their feet and the foal is nursing, you can prepare a warm bran mash for the mare. Use a little honey with some grain and chopped apple or carrots to make it more palatable.

After the foal has nursed well, it would be a good idea to milk the mare and freeze some colostrum in case you should have an orphaned foal during the season. Frozen colostrum should be thawed slowly at room temperature.

All of the above is the norm, but can vary with individual mares.

New foal emerging from mare still in sack

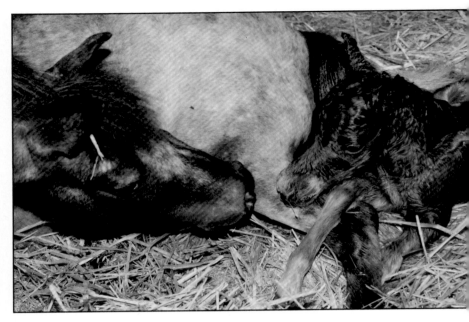

New mom greets her new foal

114

Mare urges her new baby to stand up

A shaky foal lurches to his feet

Some mares will not bag up until they deliver the foal. Some will continue to eat right up until they lie down to give birth. Most variations are probably normal for your individual mare but if you're in doubt, check with your Vet.

The placenta may be delivered with the foal but more commonly it will be passed later, within 15 minutes to two hours. Put it in a bucket of water for the Vet to examine when he comes out to check the mare and foal.

After the foal is standing, he will wobble around trying to find his first meal. This may take as long as a couple of hours. It is extremely important that he gets his mother's first milk, called colostrum, within 12 hours after birth. The colostrum not only acts as a laxative to assist the foal in passing the meconium, but contains all the necessary antibodies to give the foal immunity to disease. He will retain this immunity until approximately three months of age, at which time your Vet will probably begin his vaccine program.

Be certain the foal passes the meconium. This is a black, tarry substance which is comprised of the foal's waste products while in the uterus. If after a few hours this has not occurred, give the foal a Fleet Enema. If he still does not void, check with the Vet. It is a good idea to watch for normal urination too.

If all has been normal you should still have the Vet out to check the mare and foal within 24 hours of birth. He will check the placenta to make sure none was left inside the mare. He might give her an injection to help her uterus clean itself out. He will check her vulva for any tears or bruises which may have occurred during birth.

The foal will be checked for cleft palate, umbilical hernia and perhaps given a preventive antibiotic or tetanus injection. At this time you may want to ask the Vet what he suggests as to worming both mare and foal, and when he wants to begin the foal's vaccines.

It is not within the scope of this book to go into detail on all the problems which can occur with foaling. A good book on the subject is a wise investment and there are many to choose from. The majority of the breeders who responded to my questionnaire felt that with mares 31 inches and up, there were no more problems than with standard horse breeds. Apparently the smaller mares, 30 inches and under, are prone to more trouble. However, one breeder who has very tiny mares, down to 25 inches, has never had a problem.

To date I have lost one foal because she was apparently half way out and suffocated. She was a tiny foal (19''), out of a 34'' mare. (It was at this point that I bought the "Baby Buzzer".) The other two mares *both* needed assistance and neither were especially small nor were the foals especially large.

Handling the New Foal
Once the mare/foal relationship has been firmly established, you may begin making friends with the new baby. The sooner he becomes used to being handled, the better. Scratch him where he enjoys it most. Gently run your hands down his legs, handle his feet, and get him used to accepting your touch on all parts of his body. You may introduce him to a halter within the first few days but *do not*, under any circumstances, leave a baby, or any horse—no matter what his size or age—unattended while he is wearing a halter. Halters can get caught or snag on projections and break a neck even as you watch. I have seen it happen, so be careful!

In teaching the foal to lead, you can loop the end of the lead rope over his buttocks to help him get the idea. A few 15 minute sessions should soon have him leading like a pro. If he acts up and pulls away from you, it is better to give him slack until he calms down. These little guys should not have their heads pulled around roughly as they could be injured. See Chapter 6 for more information on handling and training.

ESTABLISHING YOUR
OWN BREEDING PROGRAM

This subject is closely related to much of the information contained in the Chapters on "Breeding" and "Purchasing a Miniature Horse for Pet, Breeding and Show". Here, however, more emphasis will be placed on genetic considerations.

Establish Your Priorities

The first step you must take is to know exactly what you want to achieve in your own breeding program. You should know the standards published by the Registries and have a thorough understanding of what makes a Miniature Horse a Miniature Horse. You should also know the type or types of Mini you want to breed.

To help you sort out your conformation goals, you may find it helpful to write down the conformation traits which are most important to you. Write these down in order of importance. This will help you to choose between individuals who are weak in some desired areas and strong in others. You will know which faults you can tolerate and which you cannot. If you have a clear picture of what you wish to achieve, selecting stock or breeding pairs will be easier.

Have Patience

From the very outset you must be aware that establishing a genetic family of animals which breed true for their good qualities and have a minimum of undesirable traits is not accomplished in a generation or two. With horses it takes much more time than with dogs or other animals who reach sexual maturity at an early age and produce several offspring per breeding cycle.

You will have to learn that you will not improve every trait you wish to in *one* breeding. If improvement in one or two traits is seen in the offspring you can consider the breeding successful. Slowly, a trait or two at a time, generation after generation, your progress can be seen. Sometimes you will encounter the inevitable setbacks, unknown genotypes will surprise you from time to time. Some may be good and some bad. You cull the bad, keep the good and keep at it.

The Importance of Keeping Records

You will find that keeping accurate written records along with photographs of each horse in your breeding program can be one of your most useful tools. If you begin with only one or two animals you may think you will remember what you need to know. Do you really think that five or six years from now, you will remember every detail about every horse you have bred, bred to, owned and/or sold?

Your records should include conformation details, good and bad, what the horse produced in its offspring, health record, foaling record including length of gestation, any foaling problems as well as height and weight of foals at birth. Include any notes which you feel could assist you in the future.

Culling and Selection

Culling and selection are two of the most important steps employed in any breeding program. The closer the breeding is genetically, the more important they become. Inbreeding especially requires ruthless culling. The lack of this can often account for the failure of some close breeding programs. You must eliminate those individuals which do not show improvement and retain those that do. In this manner the quality of your stock is constantly upgraded.

Some people equate culling with killing. This is not true. Animals can be culled by sterilization and sale. If you are well into your breeding program and consistently producing animals whose quality is well above the average of the general population, horses which you consider culls could be a strong basis for the breeding program of a newcomer. The only time I would consider death as a culling method would be in the case of a badly deformed animal or in the case of a genetically or chronically ill animal.

Setting a Type—A Line That Breeds True

If you can purchase your original breeding stock from a breeder who has consistently linebred and produced the type of animal you prefer, you will put yourself just that much farther ahead in breeding what you want. In lieu of that, perhaps you can purchase related animals from one of several breeders. If so, you are still ahead of the game.

If you can do none of the above, then buy animals which are correct in their conformation and of the type you prefer. Whether you own your own or breed to an outside stallion, make sure that he is the very best quality you can find and afford. If he is good enough to be bred back to his own daughters you have a good basis on which to begin linebreeding.

My plan is to breed for type and soundness before I go for extreme smallness. Personally I would rather have a horse who is very good in proportion and conformation and who is 33 to 34 inches in height rather than have a very small but faulty individual. If I could have both I would be ecstatic, but then, that is what we are all trying to accomplish.

I have two main goals in my personal breeding program. The first is to produce Mini's which are sound in their legs and of refined Arab type. The second is to produce small Appaloosa-type horses which are both colorful and sound.

With this in mind I have purchased two mares who came from the same sire. He has consistently produced small foals with refined bones and sound legs. My next two mares were sired by a stallion who excels in Arab type and produces beautiful Arab type heads. The next two mares are my largest, 33 and 34 inches respectively, with deep sound bodies and excellent toplines. Their heads are a bit larger than I like, but each have proven themselves to be good producers. The outside stallions selected for each mare have been of the Arab type and each has good traits where the mares are faulty.

I just recently obtained my stallion. He is 30" tall, very refined, correct in his legs and has a beautiful Arab type head with huge soft eyes. He is unrelated to any of my mares, but I already have a head start in owning two sets of half-sisters. He is a four year old and proven producer of good quality foals. His father is a very tiny, top quality horse who has been a consistent winner in the show ring.

The Appaloosa part of my program consists of a 34 inch, loud colored mare in foal to a 32 1/2 inch, loud colored stallion. The filly they produced is solid black! She has no Appaloosa characteristics at all. However, since the dam was born solid, there is still hope for color as she ages. Her conformation is excellent. Since my own stallion is so good, I will chance losing color again, and breed the Appy mare to him next.

As your own breeding program progresses keep a sharp eye out for each animal which shows significant improvement. Keep that one and, if your herd is large enough, cull the animal of the least quality. If you are consistent in this practice, your herd quality will escalate with each succeeding generation.

Inherited Problems

Since there have not been any significant research programs conducted in Miniature Horse genetics, one cannot say with certainty which problems are and are not inherited. Often a problem may crop up which is caused by environment; others are congenital. A foal's legs may be twisted within the womb and be crooked when he is born. This makes it difficult to ascertain whether or not the problem is genetically caused. This can be true of many problems and often it is wise to repeat the breeding in order to get an idea as to which is the cause.

Although specific research has not been undertaken with Mini's, I feel that it would be safe to refer to the equine research which has been done with standard sized horses. The book *Equine Genetics and Selection Procedures* has a very extensive list of inherited problems.

There are, however, several traits within the Miniature Horse Breed that do tend to act as if they are inherited.

Dwarfism

There are degrees of dwarfism, from an otherwise normal looking horse who perhaps has nostrils set very high on its muzzle to the sad little parody of an equine that can barely stand. Since dwarves are often born of normal parents, it is a trait which very probably is recessive genetically. This problem now raises the question of what to do about the parents.

A typical dwarf. This one can move about and feed itself.

If we assume that this is a genetically caused problem, then we must also assume that both parents are genetic carriers of the causative genes since neither parent was a dwarf. Since Miniature Horses are expensive, I do not think that a quick decision to cull both parents from the herd is prudent. One possibility would be to breed the mare to a different stallion and see what she produces. If the foal is again a dwarf, then I would cull the mare. The same is true of the stallion. If you do not own him do not breed to him again. If you do own him and he never produces another dwarf, you might want to continue to use him. However you must keep in mind that if he is a carrier, as his dwarf foal would indicate, he may pass the dwarf-causing genes along recessively to some of his foals and the possibility exists of those genes appearing in future generations.

But now you own a dwarf, what do you do with it? Some have ended up being advertised as the world's smallest horse and exhibited to public view. I do not feel this helps the cause of Miniature Horse breed promotion.

Some dwarves are apparently healthy and in no pain. Perhaps they could be placed in a loving home as a pet. But all should be examined by your Vet and his opinion followed as to how capable this animal is of coping with life. If he is badly deformed, I think he should be humanely euthanized. Since I have yet to face this problem it is difficult to know how I would handle it. I do know that I would never allow any animal to suffer.

Dwarves usually have extremely dished heads, nostrils placed very high on the muzzle and frequently their mouths are undershot.

Sometimes the lips appear unable to close properly over the teeth. The neck is so short that the head appears to sit directly on the body or shoulders. The body is short and the spine is often roached. The legs are very short and stubby, often deformed or twisted and clubfeet are common. The belly is often very bloated in appearance. They can display one or all of the above traits. Personally I would never use a horse with even one dwarf trait in my breeding program.

Undershot and Overshot Bites

An undershot or monkey bite is one in which the lower incisors protrude in front of the uppers. The opposite is called overshot, or parrot mouth, where the upper incisors protrude over the lower. In a normal bite the incisors meet exactly on top of each other and so do the molars. If the teeth do not occlude (meet) properly, sharp edges can develop on the molars. Since these sharp edges are not worn down properly through chewing, they continue to grow, often right into the gums causing pain, disease, and a reluctance to chew thoroughly. Since the digestive process begins in the mouth with mastication, pain during chewing will cause the horse to swallow before the food is thoroughly ground. That means the stomach must work harder than normal to digest the partially chewed food. This can result in problems such as unthriftiness and possibly colic.

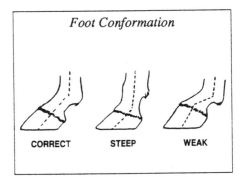

Foot Conformation

CORRECT   STEEP   WEAK

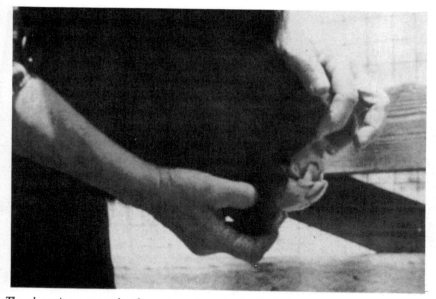

The above is an example of an extremely undershot jaw. Notice badly worn lower teeth.

This mouth is slightly overshot

It would seem that these bite problems are recessive genetic traits but *Equine Genetics and Selection Procedures* states that some authorities feel it to be a dominant allele.

Clubfeet

I was not able, in my research for this book, to locate any significant information on clubfeet. The reason I mention it here is because I have seen more examples of clubfeet in Miniature Horses than any other breed. Since we do not ride our Mini's it appears that the emphasis on sound feet and legs is not as great as in riding horses. This is really too bad because personally I find clubfeet extremely offensive.

Because it is so common in Miniatures I feel we should select and breed carefully and heavily *against* clubfeet.

I have also seen foals sired by clubfooted parents, who do not display the fault. Further observation will prove interesting.

I have also been told that clubfeet can be caused by lack of foot care or improper trimming. Maybe so but until some facts are available I intend to be very careful when breeding.

Slip Stifle (Upward Fixation Of The Patella)

This is a condition which most commonly occurs in horses with an extremely straight hind leg. When such a leg is stressed, it is more susceptible to injury than a properly angulated leg. This stress can cause the patella (knee) to slip out of place, causing the horse to display lameness, drag the leg, or walk stiffly. Once this has occurred, it is likely to recur due to the joint ligaments being stretched.

Although upward fixation of the patella can be caused by injury, its close association with a straight stifle indicates a possible genetic predisposition. It can also be caused by malnutrition and poor feeding practices. It seems to be very common in Miniature Horses.

Crooked Legs

As mentioned before, the fact that Mini's are not ridden is very probably why the quality of their legs is generally so poor. When I first became interested in buying Mini's, I found the leg quality shocking. It would appear in many cases that soundness has been sacrificed for small size.

It is my own personal opinion that this is the number one problem in Miniature Horses. There is little doubt that leg problems

This is a club foot, displaying broken angles between foot and pastern

This is a normal foot

are usually inherited although position in the womb and poor nutrition can contribute to bad legs.

Luckily there are a few horses around who are good in their legs, and these are the ones to keep in mind when breeding. More and more people are becoming interested in the performance aspect of driving their horses, and this should help improve the legs in the future since a horse with poor legs will not hold up long under the strain of pulling a cart.

When judging leg conformation, take into account the age of the animal. Two of my first Mini's purchased at very young ages, had lovely, correct legs. As their six month birthdays approached, they became badly cowhocked and toed out in front. As they neared their first year, their legs slowly began to improve until they were, once again, sound and correct. The moral to this is—don't cull too young!

Love Is Blind

In my experience with dog breeding, this is one of the most difficult problems to overcome. If it exists in the horse world, and I am sure it does, then this section belongs in this book.

When you have owned and lived with an animal, you usually fall in love with it. This is as it should be—why have them around unless we love them. But there comes a time when you feelings about your animal must be set aside. That time comes when you decide to breed. All the love you are capable of will not help produce a better animal.

I will tell you about an experience I had with Great Danes. This is a breed with many inherited problems. I do not have a kennel set up. My dogs live in the house with me and are first my friends and secondly my show dogs. I first began with Great Danes because I love the breed and their wonderful temperament. My first Dane was purchased as a pet, but then I decided to show. I located a breeder in the east and, stupidly, bought a puppy sight unseen except for photos (that is another story in itself). She not only turned out to be worse than my pet dog but was hit and killed by a car. My next purchase died of Addison's disease when he was a year and a half old.

Needless to say, not only was I disappointed, I was heartbroken. Then I bought Sunflower; I had always loved her mother and when I heard that Bambi (her mother) was to be bred, I immediately put in a reservation for a puppy. The long weeks passed, the litter was born and when she was seven weeks old I brought her home.

What a love! She was bright, full of the devil and so promising I was afraid to hope. From the beginning she was one of those special ones I knew I would always carry especially close to my heart. The older she became the more beautiful she was. She took Best of Breed and group placements in every match we attended. She was really a spectacular puppy.

Then, when she was eight months old, she was shown at her first point show: a Great Dane Specialty. The judge later told me she almost gave her the points. The next day I discovered she was a wobbler. Wobblers syndrome is a neural problem of the spine which affects gait, causing a drunken movement and lack of coordination in the hind legs and in severe cases can effect the front legs. (It also occurs in horses.) Since it is very likely genetically caused, breeding a wobbler is not a wise choice.

To express in words how I felt is impossible. I was very relieved to be told that she was in no pain and had a good chance to live a normal life. She was my love and would have been my foundation bitch. She would easily have finished her Championship. All my hopes and plans were destroyed with an x-ray. But at least she could continue to share my life.

As the months passed and Sunflower experienced her first estrus cycle I became tortured by visions of her puppies which might have been. Because she was so dear to me I had even considered breeding her and keeping the entire litter until it could be ascertained if they would become wobblers or not. But what if the ones who were not wobblers, produced it in their pups? I agonized for months over whether or not to breed her. I kept justifying it by telling myself that when she died at least I'd have one of her babies.

Probably, if I had bred her, I would never have the sound dogs I have today. I would not have begun with a sound basis: my love for her would not have affected her genotype. I spayed Sunflower and lived with her until the horrible day when I had to have her euthanized. I realize now that no dog will, or would have, ever replaced her—even her own baby. Each animal is an individual and special in their own way.

The point of this story is that if I had not been able to make an objective choice about breeding a bitch who had an inherited problem, my breeding program would not be where it is today.

129

And believe me, it was not an easy choice.

You must be able to look at your horses, dogs or whatever and see their faults right along with their assets. If you become blind to their faults through your love for them, you will do neither your own breeding program nor the breed as a whole any justice.

Leg Conformation

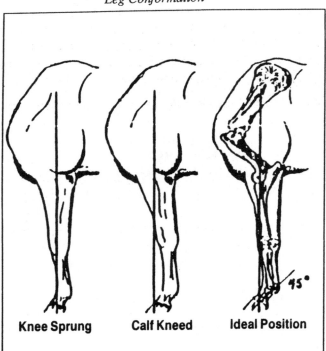

Knee Sprung   Calf Kneed   Ideal Position

OFF TO THE SHOWS

You have finally done it! You have a really good horse to show off. He is in beautiful condition, well trained and a competitive specimen. You can hardly wait to spring him on the world. So, where are the shows and what do you do?

Entering Your First Horse Show

You probably have already joined one of the Registries (see Chapter 14) with which your horses are registered. If so, you will receive lists of the shows, their dates, where they will be held, and who you should contact for further information. This is usually the Show Secretary. If you are a member of the Registry giving the show, they will mail your entry premium well before the show date. Many shows will accept entries on the day of the show at the place where the show is held, but occasionally only pre-entries are accepted. This will be stated on the premium. It usually costs less per class to pre-enter. There will be a list of classes and requirements for each. If you wish to pre-enter, decide which horse will be entered in which class and fill out the entry form accordingly. It is a good idea to make out your entry early, whether you mail it in early or post enter, since this will save time on the show day. If you have pre-entered, your exhibitor number cards will be ready and waiting for you when you arrive at the show.

Show Conditioning Your Horses

Getting your horse ready for the show begins months in advance with proper nutrition, care and grooming.

131

Braided and ready for class

Since the sunlight will quickly fade a horse's coat, you should devise a method to prevent this from occurring. The easiest method is to keep the horse in a barn or shaded enclosure during the middle hours of the day. The horse can be allowed outside before nine in the morning and after 3:30 or 4:00 P.M. to exercise and kick up its heels. At these hours the sun is unlikely to do much harm to the coat. If you have no barn, or dislike the idea of confining your horse for so many hours each day, you can have a sheet and hood made which covers the body, face and neck. The horse can also be blanketed and left outdoors at night for exercise.

If possible, try to avoid body clipping your horses. The coat is brighter and shinier when allowed to shed out naturally into the flat summer coat. Sometimes shows are held during the winter months and you either have to body clip or show the horse in its winter coat. The coat can be left long of course, but you will be at a disadvantage when competing against horses which have been clipped.

Daily brushing should be a part of your routine with your show horses. If the mane is unruly, a mane tamer should be used or the

Off to the show!

mane braided in large plaits to help it lay over. When the tail becomes long enough to almost drag on the ground, it should be braided in a long braid, rolled up, enclosed in a sock, and secured with a long rubber band. This will help keep it clean and prevent the hair from breaking off by making contact with the ground. Do not place the rubber band around the tail bone.

Grooming Your Horse For The Show

If you are planning to bodyclip your horse, do it one or two weeks before the show. This will give the coat time to grow out enough to cover any clipper marks you may have left and the coat will appear more natural. The day before the show, complete your clipping by finishing off the feet, face, and ears.

Bathe the horse using a mild shampoo and a whitener shampoo for large areas of white. Scrub the hooves well with a stiff brush. Take a clean sponge or cloth and clean the eyes, ears and nostrils. You might want to spray the mane, tail, and coat with one of the many available silicone sprays on the market. This helps keep dirt out of the hair and the mane and tail will not tangle. The spray can be applied while the coat is wet. Make sure the feet are properly trimmed, preferably three-four days before the show.

After the horse is completely dry, put on a blanket or sheet and put him into a clean stall.

Show Day

Before this exciting day dawns you would be wise to gather all the equipment you will need to take with you. A small tack box is a good investment. You will need all of your brushes and grooming equipment. Include: Hoof polish in either black or clear, rags and sponges, safety pins, baby oil, hair polish, show halter and lead rope, buckets, stable halter and lead rope, sheet or blanket, and something to spread on the ground for the horses to stand on while their feet are being polished and are drying. Plan to arrive at the show at least one hour, preferably two, before your first class. If at all possible, take a friend along to help out. There is much to do before you walk into the class.

When you arrive at the show grounds try to set up and tie your horses as close to the ring as possible. This will save you much running back and forth, and you will be aware of which classes are in the arena while you are grooming.

Your first task after seeing to your horses' comfort is to make out and pay for your entries if you have not pre-entered. If you have pre-entered, you will only have to obtain your exhibitor numbers. Unless you have a permanent card, you will need to have your horse measured.

Stand your horse on the board or rug or whatever you brought for the purpose and apply the hoof polish to a clean hoof. Keep him on the rug until the polish is completely dry.

Just before your class is called, brush out the mane, tail, body and apply a very light film of baby oil or vaseline, around the nostrils, muzzle, eyes and inside of the ears. Put on the show halter which has been polished and cleaned the day before, snap on the show lead and you are ready.

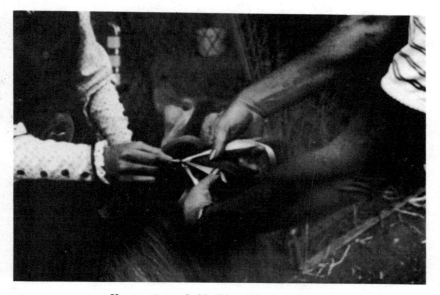

Have assistant hold ribbon when you begin.
Lay one strand of ribbon along each strand of mane.

Take time before your class to observe the judge's ring procedure. Although the ring steward will instruct you in what to do beforehand, it is helpful to see his methods for yourself. Do exactly as instructed at the gaits instructed. When you line up with the other horses, watch the judge so you will never put yourself between the judge and your horse. It is a very good idea to attend shows without your horses and observe the handlers so you will have a good idea of how to

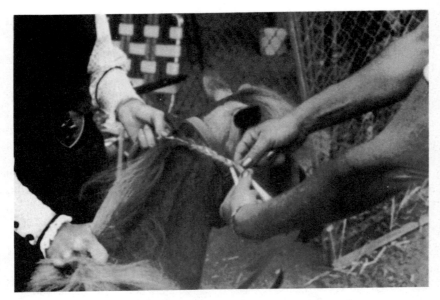

Braid along full length of hair and beyond.

Secure end by wrapping 1 strand of ribbon around braid end and inserting it back through loop. Pull snug.

behave and what to wear in the ring. You should be as well-groomed as your horse. Time and experience are your best teachers.

When the class placements are announced, receive your award in a gracious manner. If your horse has failed to place that day, you must not be a poor loser. Congratulate the winner in a sincere manner. If you feel your horse should have done better, you have every right to ask the judge why you were placed as you were. Just remember to be polite when you speak to the judge and wait until he takes a break. Neither judge nor the other exhibitors will appreciate you holding up the classes while you voice your complaints. Most judges are happy to answer your questions if they feel you are sincere and want to learn.

Horses win and lose for many reasons. Perhaps your horse is not of a "type" the judge likes. Maybe your horse acted up or you constantly obstructed the judge's view of your exhibit. Maybe your horse did not show well on that day or perhaps there were better horses competing against you. Use each show as a learning situation for yourself and your horse and you cannot help but improve.

Use the shows not only as a proving ground for your horses's quality but as a place to learn, meet fellow exhibitors and just have a good time. If your only reason for attending shows is to win, you are not going to last long in the horse business. No one wins every time—not even the best.

Driving class, lined up awaiting judges decision.

137

Nicely collected competitor in driving class.

Here's a competitor in trail, negotiating the bridge.

MINIATURE HORSE REGISTRIES

Not long ago there existed so many Miniature Horse Registries that most of us were going broke just trying to keep our stock registered with all of them. The reason for doing so was the uncertainty of which would finally prevail. Today there exist only two: the American Miniature Horse Registry and the American Miniature Horse Association.

The oldest of the two is the *American Miniature Horse Registry* which is associated with the Shetland Pony Registry. This is a *closed* registry which means that no horse may be registered unless it's parents are registered. It has been in existence since 1971, re-opened itself to horses whose parents were not AMHR registered in 1984 and then reclosed. It's publication is the *Pony Journal* which includes information on ponies as well as Miniature Horses. The address is 218 East Fifth Street, P.O. Box 435, Fowler, Indiana 47944.

The *American Miniature Horse Association* is the final outcome of the merger of Equuleus, a Florida based registry, and the International Miniature Horse Registry, based in California. The final merger took place in 1985 and the registry has been going strong ever since.

This registry is an *open* registry. This means a horse may be registered even though it's parents are not. Their publication is the *Miniature Horse World,* published six times a year. Although based in Texas, this registry approves shows all over the

United States with a National Show held yearly. The address is American Miniature Horse Association, P.O. Box 129, Burleson, Texas 76028.

Many people do not fully understand the significance of closed and open registries. There is also much disagreement as to which is most desirable. I'll try and clarify this while stating my own opinion.

The purpose of a closed registry is to maintain the purity of a breed which has already achieved the bulk of the objectives within a Standard of Perfection. If you think of a population of animals as having a "gene pool," or being carriers for all the genes needed to continue improving the breed, perhaps this will make more sense. A breed which has all the necessary traits within the gene pool, can safely have it's registry closed and still be able to forge ahead toward perfection. Numbers of animals should not be the criteria for closure; the quality of those animals, as well as their numbers must be taken into consideration.

Although many horses are presently registered with the American Miniature Horse Association (AMHA) probably *very few* are actually under the height limit of 34 inches and fewer still would be considered above average specimens. For too long, too many poor quality animals have been used within some breeding programs, and it has only been very recently that true improvement has become evident within the breed. Until a greater percentage of our registry contains really top quality animals, closing the registry would be the kiss of death for the Miniature Horse.

I would also like to see a "breeding stock" division within the registry so breeders wouldn't have to lie about the size of their over-size stock. Many mares over the 34" height, have a great deal to contribute to the breed. Mares of this size are often much more "horse-like" in their conformation than their shorter cousins. Trying to breed color, such as the Appaloosa, also brings genes for large size due to The Appaloosa's probable origination with POA's (a pony breed of Appaloosa coloring standing around 13 hands high). Just because a mare stands 38" tall, does not mean that she cannot produce a foal which will mature under 34" if bred to the right stallion.

The Registries have much useful information. They are a source of information about Mini standards, shows and breeds.

American
MINIATURE HORSE
Registry
P.O. Box 3415 — Peoria, Illinois 61614

Miniature Horse Clubs

VETERINARY OPINIONS

As with the breeders, I also sent a questionnaire to four Veterinarians who either breed Miniature Horses or who were highly recommended by Miniature Horse breeders. All had more experience with Miniature Horses than the average equine practitioner. Of the four, I received two responses. The questions and their answers follow:

1. Do you feel the Miniature Horse is generally as healthy as horses of standard size?

Both answered yes and one went on to mention the fact that lameness in Miniature Horses is almost-non existent, a situation which can be attributed to the fact that Miniature Horses are not ridden.

2. What type of feeding program do you recommend for Miniature Horses? Do you recommend hay, pellets, cubes (grain) Vitamins or other supplements? How much by weight and which brands?

Feed alfalfa or alfalfa with grass hay when available. Pelletized hay with 31% grain may be fed to those horses with "Hay Belly" problems. The disadvantage of pellets is that they are eaten quickly and do not give as much chewing time as hay. Pellets were suggested for those Miniature Horses with poor dental occlusion since they are unable to chew hay properly, making them prone to impaction colics.

3. How do you scale down vitamin supplement amounts from standard size horses to use for Miniatures?

Vitamins are unnecessary with good quality feed the Vets said. Grain and vitamins were recommended for breeding and show stock—the amount to be given is determined by the weight of the animal.

4. Do you think that the "Hay Belly" syndrome so often seen in Miniature Horses is caused by inheritance or poor management? Can it be controlled? How?

Certain "lines" have a tendency to have "Hay Bellies". Those responding said they have had fair results by feeding pelleted hay and alfalfa leaves plus exercise.

5. What products, methods and schedule do you recommend for worming Miniatures? Are certain chemicals such as organophosphates dangerous to use with Miniatures? How do you scale down the dosage?

All common paste wormers used for standard size horses are acceptable for Mini's. The dose is given according to the weight of the Mini. One doctor routinely tube wormed his horses having tubed one Miniature 22" tall. Size, age and pregnancy status are important considerations.

6. Do you recommend tube worming for Miniature Horses? Why?

One Vet said tubing was unnecessary when a proper paste worming program was faithfully adhered to.

7. At what age do you suggest a Miniature mare should first be bred?

Depends on size and conformation. Some can be bred safely at two years and some are a risk at four years. Majority breedable at three years.

8. What do you feel to be the ideal size for a Miniature brood mare? Why?

This depends on conformation. A "deep bodied" mare of 29" may be of less risk than a "tucked up" mare standing 32". As a general rule the larger the mare, the fewer the problems. It was suggested that a novice breeder purchase a mare 32"-34" tall.

9. Do you think a Miniature mare can be too small for breeding? What size is too small?

I am sure one can be too small but do not know what size. Somewhere nature will put a stop to decreasing size.

10. What problems, conformation-wise, do you feel are most prevalent in the Miniature Horse breed today? Do you think these are genetic problems?

Dwarves—have too many major dental problems. Dwarfism— overall syndrome or only a few traits such as bad mouths, big heads, bad legs etc. At this point the genetic make-up of the animal (dwarves) is unknown. Some lines of Mini's produce dwarves more frequently than others. Have seen a dwarf mare bred to a normal stallion who produced a normal foal. One of the problems is that a "breeder" who will use a dwarf stallion is also the individual who will deny doing so.

11. What are the most important traits to look for in a potential brood mare?

Look for the same qualities as in a standard sized brood mare: Depth of body is probably more important in the Miniature than in a large horse.

12. When a Miniature mare is Vet checked for breeding sound-ness, what tests should be or can be done?

Speculum exam of reproductive tract during "heat". Best to go by Veterinarian recommendation for individual horse at the time.

13. When purchasing a potential herd stallion, what tests should be covered in the Vet check?

Physical exam, external palpation of testicles, semen evaluation, evaluation of libido.

14. What is the earliest recommended age for breeding a stallion?

Three years/two years—a young stallion should be handled by an experienced person. Some stallions are not ready to breed until four or five years of age.

15. If a stallion stands at public stud what tests should the owner have done and how often?

Semen evaluation and culture several times during breeding season.

16. Do you recommend periodic sperm counts and cultures on publicly standing stallions?

Vet Number One:
Yes.

Vet Number Two:
Do not feel a sperm count is indicated unless a stallion is having a problem settling mares. A culture may be indicated on occasion, but it may make more sense to culture incoming mares.

17. Is there any accurate method to test for early pregnancy in the Miniature mare? What is it?

Uterine Ultrasound/Rectal palpation of uterus if mare is large enough and Vets hand and arm are small enough. Blood tests are useful but false results are possible. Ultrasound needs further research.

18. Do Miniature mares have any special problems foaling?

Yes—almost always related to size.

19. Should dwarf foals be allowed to live? Why or why not?

Vet Number One:
Some dwarves can function quite well and will make excellent pets for someone unconcerned with conformation. Others should be put down at once.

Vet Number Two:
Dwarves should be euthanized because every time someone sees one and relates it to a Mini, the breed suffers.

20. What causes Dwarfism?

Believed to be a recessive gene.

21. Should parents producing a dwarf be rebred to each other? Why?

No.

22. What causes the limited life span in dwarves?

They are a mutation to start with. The exact causes are unknown.

23. Do dwarves suffer? How?

Some do. Have seen some that cannot stand or eat unassisted.

24. Do you think that the following problems are genetically caused?

Clubfoot—50% of the time. Can be hereditary but may also be caused by improper foot care.

Faulty legs—50% of the time. Can be hereditary but may also be caused by inferior foot care.

Short necks—Yes.
Infertility
Vet Number One:
Yes, 50% of the time.
Vet Number Two:
Usually not—exception being retained testicles.
Under/Over—shot mouth
Yes.

25. Which vaccines and what frequency do you recommend for Mini's? At what age should babies be vaccinated?

Encephalomyelitis—Eastern and Western, Influenza, Tetanus given at 8, 12 and 16 weeks for foals with a yearly booster. Rhinopneumonitis about four times yearly. Rabies in areas with high incidents or when recommended by Veterinarian.

I recently had an experience which makes an interesting addition to this Chapter.

Upon returning home after work I discovered Streaker, my 11 day old colt rolling and thrashing on the ground in agony. He would try to stand but his rear was so weak he would simply topple over. When the Veterinarian arrived, his first suspicion was a torsion of the intestines (the gut twists back on itself making it impossible for food to pass through the intestines or blood to flow normally through veins and arteries) or a blockage of some kind. Surgery was indicated but we had a real problem. The standard equine anesthetic machine was far too powerful for a Miniature colt and the trachea tube, even foal size, would never fit into the tiny air passage.

I suggested contacting my small animal Veterinarian to ask if we could have the use of his facilities. While the two Veterinarians conferred by telephone, the small animal man suggested doing a barium series to try locating the problem site. This is a routine procedure for the small animal practitioner. It is not used with standard equines because of the impossibility of obtaining clear radiographs through the bulk of the standard horse's barrel. Streaker was bundled up and off we went to Aaron's small animal hospital.

The barium series showed very slow movement through the intestines indicating a partial intestinal blockage. This was causing the intestines to rapidly fill with gas and John (the equine Vet) and Aaron decided to operate. The trachea tube, catheters and small animal instruments proved to be the perfect size for my colt. They found a small obstruction of hay and cleared it by palpation. Watching these two talented men pool their respective knowledge for the benefit of my little colt was exciting. More importantly, it became clear that without the collaboration and cooperation between them, Streaker would very probably have died. It would seem that either equine Veterinarians are going to need to invest in smaller anesthetic machines and instruments, or perhaps there can someday be practitioners who specialize in our small breed. The above incident causes me to wonder how many Mini's have died because of lack of proper equipment.

Unfortunately, the saying which goes, "the operation was a success but the patient died," applies here. About a week after the surgery the colt again went into colic. He was hospitalized and the same day he went into convulsions. At that time I told the Vet to euthanize him.

The autopsy showed that the intestine was completely closed at the site of the previous obstruction. There were also a multitude of adhesions which extended about three feet along the intestine past the obstruction. Additionally, two ulcers were present in the stomach, probably due to the stress of the surgery. There had also been some kidney involvement. John was perplexed at the amount of adhesions since he didn't feel that the intestines had been handled enough during the surgery to cause them. I suppose it's just one of those strange mysteries that will never be solved. We did the best we could.

AFTERWORD

There are a number of changes in this second edition. The changes within the industry have been major ones. We've taken a necessary step toward consolidation of the registry and have greatly strengthened the American Miniature Horse Association (AMHA). The number of enthusiasts, owners, and exhibitors has increased tremendously and continues to do so.

I believe that the Miniature Horse is truly the breed of the future and hope that this book will help to make that future Mini as good as he can be.

I would like to extend my sincere thanks to all of you who took the time to respond to my questionnaires and also to the many of you who took time to answer my questions by phone. To those of you who encouraged me to keep going, my thanks, as well as to all of you who have been so enthusiastic about the book and have constantly recommended it to your friends making this second edition necessary!

I continue to welcome questions and comments from any of you needing help. You may contact me through my publisher Glastonbury Press, P.O. Box 1750, Ojai, CA 93024. Good luck to you all in your continued quest to improve and promote the breed of the Miniature Horse.

Author, Jill Swedlow Coffey, with Sunnyside Farm's Mini "Butterfly" and her puppy "Garfield"

About the Author
Jill speaks about herself...

I am a second generation Californian and have loved and been involved with animals almost since birth! Had I been allowed, I would have run my own private zoo as a child, but most of that had to await maturity.

When I was a kid, I used to dream that I had very tiny, living horses to play with. This dream also had to wait it's turn. I did, however, have a horse of my own from the age of 12 on and continue to have horses now -- all miniatures today!

At the time I began in Miniatures, I was certainly no novice in the horse field. I have owned, shown, and bred horses for many years.

I have also owned, bred, and shown Great Dane dogs for almost 17 years. Several home-bred champions give evidence of a well-planned breeding program.

Other interests of mine include computers, (oh what did we ever do without word processing?!!?) gardening, music, photography, and art, and of course --writing-- to name just a few!

Several of my horses have won championships and reserve championships in conformation and driving. My present breeding program is heading in the direction which I have envisioned. I guess my advice worked even for me!

The following is
a breeder's listing.
It includes some of
the breeders from
the United States
and Great Britain.

THISTLEDOWN FARM

Miniature Horses

HOME

   OF . . .

BOND ANTHONY
31"

1986 Palomino Stallion-

BOND CHAUNCEY
31-1/2"

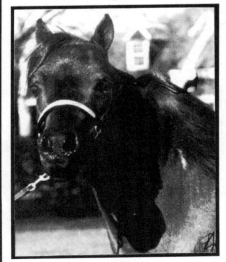

1977 Bay Stallion

**Producing & Promoting
Quality Registered
MINIATURE
HORSES**

**Franklin W. McCann, Owner
119 Botsford Hill Road
Bridgewater, CT
06752
(203) 354-4628**

Peggy Wilson, Manager

1990 AMHR National Grand Champion All Star
"STAR FARMS WHITNEY'
1989 Mare 28"

1990 Show Record

5 AMHR SHOWS GCMHC
· 20 First Place Wins
· Multi-Grand & Reserve Jr. Mare
· Supreme Halter Horse
· 1990 Grand Champion High Point GCMHC in:
      Yearling Mares
      Solid Color
      Youth Mares
      Stock Class
1990 AMHR National All Star Grand Champion Jr. Exhibitor In-Hand
1990 AMHR National All Star Grand Champion Solid Color
1990 AMHR National All Star Top Ten (4th) Yearling Mare

7 AMHA SHOWS MHCSC
· 7 First Place Wins
· 6 Grand Champion Jr. Mare
· 1 Reserve Champion Jr. Mare
· Liberty Class Winner
· 1990 AMHA National Qualifier
· 1990 Grand Champion High Point Yearling Mare

HOME OF 'PROVEN' CHAMPION QUALITY FILLIES AND COLTS
SETTING THE STANDARD OF QUALITY

MARILYN ERB
Owner

FUN IN THE SUN
MINIATURE HORSES

(619) 579-6527

5266 GRANDRIDGE RD., EL CAJON, CA 92020

All Time Top Winning Miniature Horse
in the Northwest Region 1991.....
Del's Benny

This exquisite little stallion is indeed a **Super <u>Star!</u>**
He began his show career at age eleven and excelled to many
times Grand Champion, Supreme Halter Horse and High
Point Performance Horse. He has received numerous special
awards including AMHA.

At the miniature horse nationals he received TOP TEN
placements each of the four years he attended.

In 1989 he was National Reserve Champion Senior Stallion
in his halter class. Now at fifteen, he stands very proud and is
truly a fine example of the breed. He has done it all!

TOYHORSE INTERNATIONAL

GREAT BRITAIN
Est. 1965 / Pedigrees From 1864
Heights From 23", All Colors

Toyhorse Treacle - Yearling Colt - Now enjoying life in the U.S.A.

British Bred Miniatures With Pedigrees
Up to 125 Years Officially Recorded

Annual Production Sale Every October.

Tiny friendly mini-equines, bred to give pleasure to young and old alike.
Toyhorses can now be seen world-wide and continue to excel in the
showing all the way from Australia through Europe to the United States.

Visitors by Appointment - Just call (from U.S.A. 011 44) 40 382 2639 to
arrange a visit this summer. Many inexpensive guest houses near-by
and 100 foals due from May onwards. London/Gatwick Airport thirty
minutes distance.

British Agent for Miniature Horse Equipment
"Driving Courses" Every Autumn and "Open Days"

Tikki Adorian, Howick Farm, The Haven
Billingshurst, West Sussex, RH 14 9BQ, Great Britain
TEL 011-44-403-872-2639   FAX 011-44-403-872-2014

Firelight's Mc Nugget

Stallion, 30³/4", foaled 1982

Grandsire: Helium
Sire: Firelight of Marshwood (31¹/4")
Granddam: Claribel

Grandsire: Freeman's Red Man (28¹/2")
Dam: Firelight's Nugget (33")
Granddam: McCoy's Anne (Smith McCoy mare)

"Mac" is an example of the type of Miniature we strive to produce; small, correct, refined, with intelligence and good disposition. He also has solid foundation breeding. Our broodmare band, though not large, was carefully selected, mare by mare, for their fine qualities and backgrounds.

Foals and older stock available. Visitors always welcome by appointment.

Helen and Allan Marble, Thistle Meadow Farm
12 Duval Road, Dudley, Mass. 01571   Phone (508) 764-8366

Falabella:
The world's original breed of miniature horse.

Thanks to the ackowledgement of the Argentine government and the Asociacion Argentina de Fomento Equinos only miniature horses from the Establecimientos Falabella (owned by Maria Luisa de Falabella) can be exported from Argentina as authentic Falabella miniature horses.

Horses for sale and import.
Top Argentine and American Bloodlines.

BLUEBELL HOLLOW

Ronnie and Jean Bullock
7625 W. Bailey Run Rd.
Millfield, Ohio 45761
(614) 797-2300
Located near
Athens, Ohio

dc's
CHOCO-LITE
32 1/2" Stallion
Chocolate
with flaxen
mane & tail
"Choco" is a
"Here I am! -
Look at me!"
Charmer

MINIATURE HORSES
MINIATURE AUSTRALIAN SHEPHERDS
AND OTHER ANIMALS

TOYLAND

Toyland Zodiac 31" Pure Falabella Stallion.
Rare Leopard Appaloosa
Sire: Boone's HFS Macho 32½" (Imported Falabella)
Black Leopard Appaloosa.
Dam: HFS Carmen 31" (Imported Falabella) Black.

A Few Bred Mares & Foals by Zodiac. Others available.

The Falabella Miniature Horse

The **"FALABELLA"** Miniature Horse is a "PURE STRAIN" which is directly IMPORTED, OR OUT OF IMPORTED LINES with all Ancestors tracing their origin to the FALABELLA FARMS IN ARGENTINA. PURE FALABELLA STOCK is very rare and highly valued. Only PURE FALABELLA'S may be registered with the **FMHA,** (Falabella Miniature Horse Association) which authenticates their purebred ancestry. Many breeders consider it highly desirable to acquire PURE FALABELLA stock to produce the *pure strain* or to cross with their American stock. The PURE FALABELLA strain gives better value to the foals and is known to reduce size as well. Within the Miniature Horse industry, The FALABELLA is one of the most prestigious to own.

Top American Lines	**American/Falabella Blends**	**Pure Falabella Stock**
"Starter Packages"	Investment Packages All Colors	Delivery World-Wide

RODABI-J RANCH

Rodabi-J Backcountry Bay
(Photo by Lindalee M. Akin)

Rodabi-J Ranch - - - Home of REH'S PATRIARCH

Barbara Naviaux
P.O. Box 144, Placerville, CA 95667, (916) 622-1040

Photo courtesy of: Bloomington Herald-Telephone

We're Little, But We're Good!

Registered Miniature Horses
from

IONA
MINIATURE HORSE FARM

Stock For Sale
Visitors Welcome by Appointment

Bonnie & Gordon Harris
Owners
(513) 836-2565

7320 Wastler Rd.
Clayton, OH 45315

Running Creek Miniatures

NFC's Ace High 32½"
Sire: Flying W Farms Meadow Muffin 28"

Ace is a proven color producer.
His 1989 foals are due starting in March.

1989
Stud Fee
$500.00

Owned by:
Garry and Linda Williams
26904 Rd. 13
Elizabeth, Colorado 80107
(303) 648-3181

THE ARITHMETIC IS RIGHT!!

CHAMPION

Majestic Tiger's Challenge 29-1/4"
Multi-Grand Champion Stallion
"CHAD"

CHAMPION

Glory Be Farm's Fortune Cookie 32"
1990 AMHA National Grand Champion
Youth & Top Ten Senior Mare
Multi-Supreme & Grand Champion

EQUALS

Gypsy Magic's Capital Gain
MAMHS Futurity Champion Colt

"Cappy" is just one of our *DYNAMITE* 1991 Foals.
Our Congratulations to His New Owner
Leatherstocking Miniatures
Fly Creek, New York

A SINCERE "THANK YOU" TO...
...Our Special Clients for Making 1991 a Year To Remember
...The Purchasers of our 1991 "Babies"
~~~THE CHAMPIONS OF TOMORROW~~~

Gypsy Magic Miniature Horse Farm

10504 Vincent Road • White Marsh, Maryland 21162

Bob & Leslie Kaminski
(301) 574-5255
Tom & Stephanie Welsh
(301) 335-8678

Just Bronco (28³/4", Buckskin)

1988 Reserve National Champion, Solid Color Stallions

A proven champion with many blues in, Mature Stallions 28" to 30", Solid Color Stallions, Mature Stallions, Halter Obstacle and was Norcal's 1988 Hi-Point Stallion, 28 to 30 inches.

Just Bronco - The mark of a truly great sire; beauty, proudness in his eyes, conformation, color, size, balance and the ability to pass this on to his offspring.

Steve & Kim Sterchi

Owned by: 16242 Tierra Road
Grass Valley, CA 95949
(916) 268-0568

Landry's Charlie Boy

Chianti (33") (Falabella, loud leopard)
Shadow Oak's Cock Robin (30^1/$_2$") (Appy, blanketed sorrel)
Vanilla 3rd (33^1/$_2$") (Appy, blanketed sorrel)
Landry's Charlie Boy
Pistol's Casey Branaman (29^1/$_2$") (Bay)
Fisher's Melinda (33^1/$_2$") (Sorrel)
Fisher's Melody (33")

Iles' This & That Farm
LeRoy and Evelyn Iles
5161 Mosherville Rd.
Jonesville, MI 49250
(517) 563-2856

GOLD HILL

Presents
BOND ROLLBACK
Senior Herd Sire

Lindalee M. Akin
550 Gold Hill Road
Placerville, Ca 95667
(916) 622-6968

Telephone Inquiries Preferred

FALLEN STAR RANCH

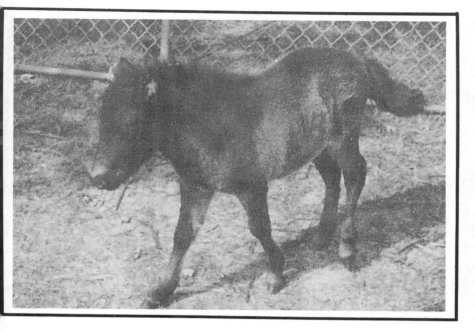

Fallen Star's Iza (Bond Triumph X Georgia's Black Beauty)
One of the 1988 foals. 18" at birth

'endell and Carol Lowery
t. 4, Box 197
astman, Georgia 31023

AMHA Reg. Minature Horses
(912)374-3111 or
(912)374-2658

Quality and honesty are the watchwords at Sunnyside Farm. Whether you're just beginning, want to improve your herd, or looking for a loveable pet, we're here to help. Our interest and assistance continues after the sale. Call or write for Sales Lists and Stallion Lists. Please call ahead for an appointment. We are only fifteen minutes off of the 10 freeway and within thirty minutes of a major airport.

SUNNYSIDE FARM

GREAT DANES AND MINIATURE HORSES

Jill Swedlow
39887 Swedlow Trail
Yucaipa, California 92399
(714) 797-1855

SUNNYSIDE STALLIONS

Komoko's Black Devil, "Danny" 32"

Komoko's Little Champ 26¹/2"
Komoko's Black Jack 30"
Komoko's Sandy 29¹/2"
Komoko's Black Devil 32"
Komoko's Sundance 29 ¹/2"
Komoko's Miss Hi-Lo 30"
Komoko's Eve 33"

Danny is a top sire at Sunnyside, having proven himself as a producer of National Champion get. He is prepotent for his fantastic head, type and temperament. Danny is a rare blood bay. He has won numerous Halter and Driving Championships. He is at stud to approved mares.

SUNNYSIDE STALLIONS

Fantasy Dream Maker "Flash" 30.25"

Bond Sir Galahad 27¹/₂"
Bond Apollo 28¹/₂" (National Champion)
Bond Samantha 32"
Fantasy Dream Maker 30¹/₄"
Unknown
Sligo Crissy 34"
Hobbyhorse Fancy 34"

Flash is an unusually marked, bay pinto with four stockings. He has won multiple Grand Champion Stallion titles. More exciting are his foals! Very small, correct legs, extreme arab-type heads, and he's producing some *very unusual*, striking markings. One son was National top ten out of a class of almost eighty weanlings.

SUNNYSIDE STALLIONS

Bond Adonis 27³/₄"

Bond Showboy 28¹/₂"
Bond Shadrack 28"
Bond Leander 32"
Bond Adonis, 27 ³/₄"
Bond Sir Galahad 27¹/₂"
Bond Hankering Hannah 29"
Bond Coco 30"

Adonis, a slate and white pinto, is the most correct, SMALL Mini I've ever seen. He moves beautifully and is a proven sire of excellent, tiny, colored and solid foals. Himself an AMHA National Champion, he is also a producer of champions. He is available to outside approved mares.

SUNNYSIDE MARES

Sunnyside Dots Enough 32"

Sunnyside Iben Spotted (33")
Komoko's Black Devil (32")
Shadow Oaks Ribbon (33 1/2")
Sunnyside Dots Enough (32")
Unknown
Sunnyside Lotta Dots
Unknown

Nuffie is a 3/4 sister to Dots Incredible. She has done very well in the show ring. Double Appaloosa bred, she should make a great broodmare.

SUNNYSIDE MARES

Komoko's Fantasy Mercedes 29¹/₂"

Komoko's Whiskey Sour 26"
Komoko's Acey-Ducey 26¹/₂"
Komoko's Misty 29"
Komoko's Fantasy Mercedes 29¹/₂"
Komoko's Little Champ 26¹/₂"
Komoko's Little Kimbo 28¹/₂"
Komoko's Little Pocahontas 29"

Garnering Grand Champion Mare every time out, this mare is undefeated. She combines qualities difficult to find in such a small mare; pretty head, good legs and overall excellent conformation. Best of all, she's producing her great qualities in her get.

Sunnyside Mares

Sunnyside Dots Incredible 33"

Komoko's Black Jack 30"
Komolo's Black Devil 32"
Komolo's Miss HI-Lo 30"
Sunnyside Dots Incredible 33"
Unknown
Sunnyside Lotta Dots 33 1/2"
Unknown

Dots is the most exciting foal ever born at Sunnyside. She has lived up to her name, being undefeated in Color Mare, including 1988 AMHA National Champion Color Mare. She has also done great in Halter, having placed first 5 times and 2nd once. She was the SoCal Hi-Point Color Mare and Halter Filly and Dots *really* Incredible.